Positive Realism

Positive Realism

Maurizio Ferraris

Winchester, UK
Washington, USA

First published by Zero Books, 2015
Zero Books is an imprint of John Hunt Publishing Ltd., Laurel House, Station Approach,
Alresford, Hants, SO24 9JH, UK
office1@jhpbooks.net
www.johnhuntpublishing.com
www.zero-books.net

For distributor details and how to order please visit the 'Ordering' section on our website.

Text copyright: Maurizio Ferraris 2014

ISBN: 978 1 78279 856 9
Library of Congress Control Number: 2015932894

A CIP catalogue record for this book is available from the British Library.

Design: Lee Nash

Printed and bound by CPI Group (UK) Ltd, Croydon, CR0 4YY, UK

We operate a distinctive and ethical publishing philosophy in all
areas of our business, from our global network of authors to
production and worldwide distribution.

CONTENTS

Prologue

Strong, independent, stubborn: that's the world of objects surrounding us (but also of the subjects we interact with). We cannot change the world (or people, for that matter) at will – that's why change is so hard to achieve. Yet, this world does not just say no – it doesn't merely resist us as if to say, "here I am, I'm here." With the same gesture with which it resists us, it also gives us access to the greatest and only positivity at our disposal: that is, the background (far from amorphous, but rather rich and structured) from which sensations, imagination, thinking, memory, expectation, fear and hope arise. Indeed, from its very negativity this world unfolds all possibilities, in accordance with Hamlet's saying that there are more things between heaven and earth than are dreamt of in our philosophies. In what follows, I will reflect on six words: Invite, Resistance, Objects, Realism, Fiction and Possibility. In doing so I will try to outline – in a very preliminary way – the characters of this positivity which we all rely on and yet do not think about (to the point that it seems to be forgotten by philosophy, which seems to care very much about thought, but very little about the world).

My starting point, in a nutshell, is a thought experiment. Let's adopt Husserl's *epoché* and suspend for a moment Kant's Copernican revolution, to follow – as far as possible – a hypothesis: the coexistence and interaction of different beings in the world depend primarily on the properties of the latter, and not on the conceptual schemes of the 'I think', (which, in Kant's perspective, seems charged with hyperbolic responsibility). In short, if we want a Copernican revolution, let's do it for real. So, instead of placing Man at the centre of the universe like Kant did, let's turn him/her into a secondary spectator of a world that is much greater and older than s/he is.

Awakening from the transcendentalist slumber does not

mean embracing naive realism (which identifies experience with reality), or a metaphysical realism, which views the mind as the mirror of nature. It is, instead, a deconstructive gesture: if deconstruction is the ability to challenge the *doxa*, prejudice and lazy reason, then – after two centuries dominated by the refrain that language, history and concepts shape the world – it comes to doing the opposite. Of course we should acknowledge that this autonomy (and often antinomy) between the world and our perceptual apparatuses takes the form of negativity and resistance, as if it were an obstacle. But we should not forget that the world can also accommodate us, offering support, invites and resources. Above all, though, we should be aware that anyway, both in impeding us and in accommodating us, the world is given as positivity, as wealth, as an offer of objects that are much finer-grained than the concepts with which we try to demarcate them.

By "positivity" I simply mean this: the world, as Kant rightly noted, can only be thought of as a regulating idea containing the totality of all beings. Yet, we will never be able to directly experience the world, as it is too big an object for this to be possible. This element, however, suggests an initial positivity of which Kant does not seem to have thought: the fact that, despite overwhelming our conceptual schemes and perceptual apparatuses, the world *does* give itself is clear evidence of the fact that our schemes and concepts have no constitutive relation to the world – if anything, their value is only cognitive. In short, the scope of our concepts and perception is epistemological, not ontological. After all, this is a very common experience: we are born ("we come into the world") in a world that has pre-existed us from time immemorial, and we die with the awareness that this world is destined to exist for a very long time after us. Here we encounter the sense of a second positivity: being *is*, there are things in the world, and this is a character of objects, not subjects (contrary to what was posited by many philosophers in the last few centuries).

One might object – we shall see it later – that philosophy has never denied the existence of a world 'out there', and this is largely true. Indeed, some philosophers have done worse. They have pictured a world with no form, qualities or properties – a sort of cookie dough for subjects able to give it shape, meaning and use. Now, if the subject (that at best is well aware of being inept, limited, stupid and poor of imagination, memory and culture) is capable of such a thing, it is because the forms, meanings and uses are mostly *already in the world,* just waiting to be summoned by a human or an animal. This is the third positivity of the real, which Putnam refers to when he claims that meaning is not in the mind but in the world.[1] The water of Twin Earth imagined in his thought experiment, with a chemical composition $X_Y Z$, is not water, even though the natives believe that it is.

In the following pages I would like to transfer this account from epistemology to ontology: if given that the properties of the two waters, regardless of their chemical composition, are equal, then there is an even stronger sense in which the meaning is in the world. Both H_2O and $X_Y Z$ invite one to drink and bathe, suggesting a direction of use, both for humans (that at one point, thanks to epistemology, will discover that the two liquids are not the same) and for non-human beings (who probably will never know). And this doesn't only apply to physical experiences: the way in which moral value or non-value, or beauty come forward is clearly the sign of something that comes from outside, surprising us and affecting us. The world can affect us because, in fact, it lies on the outside of us – otherwise, it would be just imagination. But let's come to the keywords.

The first is *invite.* The world manifests a direction of use, a sense of flow, calls us, gives us possibilities and positivities, and gives us something that is given, not merely thought of. After all, this is the other side of pragmatism, which had the merit of insisting that our relationship with the world is not only cognitive, but involves an action on the part of the subject. The latter, in turn, does not merely contemplate the world, but uses resources, seeks solutions, transforms situations. The fact that this action is possible depends on reality, which *calls for us* – let's not forget that the Italian word for thing, "cosa", derives from the Latin "causa", but the Greek word for it is "πράγμα", from which derive "praxis", "pragmatics" and "pragmatism". It might be banal, but this banality is rich and profound: a handle invites one to handle it, and this propriety is not in the subject but in the object. It is hard not to recognize a face in a house with two windows and a door in the middle (it's the same reason why we speak of bottle *neck* and table *leg*) – after all, it's a *façade*. We might not want it, we might not think of it, but that's how it is: the world's invite is stronger than us, because the initiative lies in the object, which is not a docile amorphous bundle, but a concentration of qualities, quantities, forms, properties and mostly possibilities.

This leads me to the second word: *resistance*. The possibilities and positivities of the world do not depend on the power of the subject, let alone on thought. On the contrary, they depend on the fact that the world is recalcitrant to our will and exerts a friction against it. But, once again, there is a point that cannot be neglected: this resistance, which is subjectively perceived as negativity (the world does not correspond to our expectations), is in fact the largest source of positivity, i.e. what distinguishes reality from imagination. In fact, the first manifestation of existence is resistance, the grumpy incorrigibility of reality, which manifests itself primarily, but not exclusively, in sensible experience. If things are in this way, the first principle on which to build our philosophy, as well as our relationship with the world, is not "ego cogito, ego sum", but "it exists, therefore, it resists". Because, after all, even the cogito manifests its existence through a resistance: if it can serve as proof of existence it is precisely because it appears to itself as given, as something that we encounter in our psychic experience and that we cannot change at will.

The third word, *object* – or rather, objects, since the sphere of objectivity is constitutively plural – requires a few more lines. For positivity to come forward, it is necessary that the invite come from a real object. This applies not only to natural objects, but also to social objects, ideal objects, artefacts, feelings and events. Obviously, when a physicist investigates the properties of matter, s/he is examining matter, and not her own mind; in the same way, a mathematician struggling with a theorem is not undergoing a session of self-consciousness.

Besides, the fact that social objects – like the law or economy – are independent of human beings does not entail that they are not mysterious. If we move from the generic abstraction 'Man' to the multitude of human beings, and especially to the vast number of social objects (and now also of electronic devices) that they incessantly produce, we will see how little truth lies in Vico's saying that society is transparent because it is the product of Man. The surprises that many documents hold for us, the power they wield on the subject even beyond the intentions of the latter, the possibility – immanent in every form of writing – of initiating automatic processes beyond the control of those who created them are all evidence of the unpredictability of objects, even when they depend on the social world for their genesis (in the case of artefacts) and existence (in that of social objects).

The fourth word is *realism* – or rather, once again, the plural noun realisms, because theories are objects too. Not only are there many realisms (and new realisms), but every one of us can be a realist regarding some objects and an antirealist regarding other ones – indeed, placing tales, laws and therapies on the same level doesn't seem like a good strategy. From the perspective I'm defending, in particular, realism regarding social objects is weaker than that regarding natural objects or concrete artefacts. In fact, my view acknowledges that social objects need subjects not only for their genesis but also for their persistence: if mankind ceased to exist mountains would stay the same, but taxes, holy days and ambassadors would disappear. Not all realists share this view: suffice it to think of a speculative realist like Graham Harman and another "new realist" like Markus Gabriel (on whom I shall come back later). For them, everything – from physical to social objects – exist in the same way. This is yet another sign that realism is an open field, a sphere of positivity – that is, the opposite of unified thought.

The fifth word is *fiction*: the invite of the real permeates fiction as well. This, in my view, is the crucial side of the relationship between fiction and reality, much more than the point everyone usually insists on – that is, that reality is full of fiction or even that, either just in this day and age or since the dawn of time, the two notions are indistinguishable. Now let's suspend for a while the discourse on the aestheticization of the world and on fiction taking over reality, and let's ask ourselves a simple question: what writer could have foreseen the Thirty Years' War, Talleyrand's political career, Kutuzov's strategy or the invention of the World Wide Web? Once again, meaning lies in the world, not in the subjects. Of course, we also have to deal with the subjects involved in these historical events, but Kutuzov's strategy was nevertheless the outcome of a number of circumstances, properties, objects and subjects in the world that Tolstoy's mind would never have been able to imagine. After all, even studies on psychosis show that delirious ideations, according to patients themselves, are simply constituted by the re-composition of fragments of reality: things seen, lived, perceived are reduced to fragments and then restructured. In the end, this is exactly what Lacan claimed when he said that hallucinations are pure real, non-compromised by the symbolic order[2]: in other words, the real has its autonomous structure long before the subject comes in.

It should come as no surprise then that the last word should be *possibility*. What do possibilities derive from, if not from the contact with the real? Kant had already understood this. In his view, Leibnizians wonder whether the sphere of possibility is larger than reality and answer that yes, it has to be, because reality requires a further determination – existence. According to Kant, they are wrong because only the real exists. This may seem not to be much, or obvious, but it's far from being so. Precisely *because* only the real exists, every moment of our life is crossed by possibility and by the imagination representing it to us. This resource accompanies us for all our life and never leaves us. Those who have seen others pass away ensure that while agonizing, if the dying person speaks, she refers to real things, objects and actions: laundry to do, flowers to water, wheels to change. Or roosters to return, as in the case of Socrates, whose last words – that Nietzsche considers "ridiculous and terrible"– were "O Crito, we owe a cock to Asclepius. Do pay it. Don't forget."[3]

Bonn, 13 June 2013

Note

These are the first stages of a vaster and more systematic work to come. They are based on very recent essays I wrote in different circumstances and that focus on the positivity of the real. I re-elaborated them in Bonn thanks to the Käte Hamburger Kolleg "Recht als Kultur": my sincerest thanks to the director, Professor Werner Gephart. This is where the essays to follow come from: 1. *Invite*: my speech at the conference "Le molte facce del realismo. Geografia e storia di un problema filosofico", Milan, Università Vita-Salute San Raffaele, 17 February 2013; 2. *Resistance*: "To exist is to resist", in *Bentornata realtà*, ed. by M. De Caro and M. Ferraris, Turin, Einaudi, pp. 139-166; 3. *Objects*: my speech at the Bonner Humboldt-Preisträger-Forum "Das neue Bedürfnis nach Metaphysik" on 24 October 2012 in Bonn 4. *Realisms*: discussion on

Hilary Putnam's *Philosophy in an Age of Science* in "Iride. Filosofia e discussione pubblica". 5. *Fiction*: my speech at "Metodi Testo Realtà", Turin, Museo Nazionale del Risorgimento Italiano, 7-8 May 2013. 6. *Possibilities*: dialogue with Achille Varzi (as Philonous) held on 10 May 2013 at the Circolo dei lettori in Turin. I thank all my friends at the LabOnt that, as always, have given me precious suggestions and helpful comments. A special thanks goes to Raffaella Scarpa and Vincenzo Santarcangelo, who read my book with the same zealousness they would devote to their own work.

1

Invite

1. πράγμα.

The first essential principle of positive realism is that the world does not merely say "no": it does not only resist us. It is also the greatest ontological positivity. In order to illustrate this point I would like to consider the debate that took place roughly twenty years ago between a constructivist, Richard Rorty, and a negative realist, Umberto Eco.[4] With the aim of demonstrating the world's plasticity with regards to our vital objectives, Rorty affirmed that "one can clean one's ear with a screwdriver". This was denied by Eco, who posited that you cannot clean your ears with a screwdriver because it is too long and pointy, but you could very well use it as a weapon instead (Eco referred to the "screwdriver murders" on Italian streets in the Sixties). It is as simple as that: the constructionist claims that reality is docile in respect of our purposes, while the negative realist objects that it can also say "no" to us. Upon closer inspection however, the situation is more complex and promising than that: this very simple example is enough for us to notice that the small portion of reality we call "screwdriver" does not merely say 'no' to us but, at the same time, it offers us an invite (or rather, many invites).

Children in a pre-linguistic age are already able to segment linguistic reality into objects – which for Kant, strictly speaking, would not be possible, given that, presumably, they do not possess the scheme of substance as permanence in time.[5] These objects, in turn, have properties that constitute a set of 'invites'. By this term I mean a notion that was widely used in the twentieth century, in a timeframe that goes from phenomenology to Gestalt psychology up to Heidegger's existential analytics. The idea is that, at least to some extent, meanings are in the world, embodied in objects which offer us affordances – to use Gibson's term, [6] which has a significant precedent in Fichte's 'Aufforderungskaracter'.[7]

In short, every negation entails a determination, and every determination is a revelation. The impossibility of using a screwdriver as a glass, a needle or a cotton bud hides just as many possibilities: you can use a screwdriver as a dagger, a lever, a skewer... If this holds for an object as simple as a screwdriver, it's not hard to imagine what possibilities rest in ontologically 'richer' realities, both in the sphere of natural objects and in the sphere of social objects. Ecosystems, state organizations, interpersonal relationships: every one of these structures, infinitely more complex than a screwdriver, feature the dynamic of negation and invite. One might object that these objects are nothing without a subject able to give them some meaning, but this is precisely the point we should be most careful about: what do we mean by 'subject', to begin with? Can this notion be tolerant enough to include a superorganism like a termite mound?[8] And, if it isn't, how do we explain that a termite mound is a structure so powerful and evolutionarily successful?

2. Constructivism.

This positivity of the real goes against the constructivist mainstream of modern philosophy.[9] According to this view, we cannot access reality through immediate experience but only through knowledge, so that natural light is replaced by the sovereign enlightenment of reason, and the world, reduced to mere negativity, is conceived of as the non-I as opposed to the I – the alienation of the spirit into something that is not thought. Of course, constructivists claim that the world's dependence on conceptual schemes is not causal, but merely representational[10]: we are not the creators of the universe, but we shape it starting from an amorphous *hyle*, a cookie dough modelled by the subjects with the stamps of concepts.[11] Thus, the existence of the world is granted, but at the cost of losing the world's structural and morphological autonomy.

The 'representational dependence' of the world means that: 1) there is no world if not for a spectator (correlationism)[12] and 2) the spectator is actually the constructor of that world (constructivism). However, if we try to give concrete shape to representational dependence, we will notice that the technical term hides conceptual confusion. Following this thesis, you take a being (say, the Tyrannosaurus Rex as a physical entity) and treat it as if it were a linguistic or zoological notion, concluding that – since without humans the term 'Tyrannosaurus Rex' wouldn't exist – the Tyrannosaurus Rex 'representationally' depends on humans. Which is either a truism (if by 'representationally' we mean something like 'linguistically') or a perfect absurdity (if by 'representationally' we mean something – even slightly – more than that). In fact, this would imply that the being of the Tyrannosaurus Rex depends on us; but then, given that when the Tyrannosaurus Rex existed we did not, it would paradoxically follow that the Tyrannosaurus Rex both did and did not exist.[13] Ontology (what there is) is systematically resolved in epistemology (what we know, or think we know), just like the Tyrannosaurus Rex is systematically confused with the word 'Tyrannosaurus Rex'.

This is a consequence of what I propose to call 'transcendental fallacy', namely, the Kantian proposal to found experience through science. To achieve this, we need a change of perspective: we have to start from the subjects rather than the objects, and ask ourselves not how things are in themselves, but how they should be made in order to be known by us, following the model of physicists who question nature not as scholars, but as judges, using schemes and theorems. Kant then adopts an *a priori* epistemology, i.e. mathematics, to found ontology: the possibility of synthetic *a priori* judgments allows us to fixate an otherwise fluid reality through certain knowledge. In this way, transcendental philosophy moves constructionism from the sphere of mathematics to that of ontology. The laws of physics and mathematics are applied to reality and, in Kant's hypothesis, they are not the contrivance of a group of scientists, but they are the way in which our minds and senses actually work.

If we take ontology and epistemology to be at one, our knowledge will no longer be threatened by the unreliability of the senses and the uncertainty of induction, but the price we have to pay is that there is no longer any difference between the fact that *there is* an object X and the fact that *we know* the object X. And since for Kant – just like for Descartes and postmodern thinkers – knowledge is inherently construction, there is no difference in principle between the fact that we know the object X and the fact that we construct it – just as in mathematics, where knowing $7 + 5 = 12$ is equivalent to constructing the addition $7 + 5 = 12$. Of course, Kant invites us to think that behind the phenomenal object X there is a noumenal object Y, a thing-in-itself inaccessible to us; but the fact remains that the sphere of being coincides to a very large extent with that of the knowable, and that the knowable is essentially equivalent to the constructible.

3. Positive Philosophy.

This fallacy was clearly stigmatized by the 'second' Schelling. All modern philosophy – from Descartes to Kant and Fichte, to Schelling himself in the first phase of his thought, up to Hegel – is negative philosophy. 'Ego cogito ergo sum', 'intuitions without concepts are blind', 'what is rational is real': all these expressions mean that certainty is to be sought in epistemology, in what we know and think, and not in ontology (what there is). For the later Schelling however, the opposite direction is the one to follow. Being is not something constructed by thought: it is given before thought comes to be. Not only because we know of interminable periods in which there was the world, but there were no people, but also because what initially appears as thought actually comes from outside of us: the words of our mother, the myths and rules, the totems and taboos that we encounter in everyday life are merely found by us, just as in Mecca one comes across a meteorite.

Under the theoretical profile, ontological necessity can be articulated through the argument from facticity.[14] We build cars, use them, sell them, and this undoubtedly depends on us. Yet the *fact* that we build cars, that there were things before us and that there will be things after us does *not* depend on us. There cannot be a generalised constructivism with regard to facts, and this is because, banally, there are facts that precede us: we could all say, like Erik Satie, "I have come into the world very young into an era very old". In this world that is given to us, "we follow the rule blindly", as suggested by Wittgenstein: that is – translating this formula into our terms – we rely on an ontology that precedes epistemology, or on a competence that precedes understanding.

We encounter objects that have an ontological consistence independently from our knowledge and that then, either suddenly or through a slow process, are known by us. We find out parts of ourselves (for instance, that we are envious or that we have fear of mice) just like we discover pieces of nature. We notice elements of society (for instance, enslavement, exploitation, women's subordination and then, with a greater sensitivity, also mobbing or political incorrectness) that turn out to be unbearable and were previously hidden, namely assumed as obvious by a political or social unconscious. This encounter does not amount to acceptance. The moment of awareness will hopefully come, but it will be a matter of acknowledging what we are and what the world is. In the psychological and social world, the motto could be 'I am therefore I (sometimes) think'. And what I think is not the result of an absolute, constitutive and independent intentionality, but of a documentality made of traditions, languages and influences that draw the psychic world no less than the social.[15]

4. Emergence.

Under the historical profile, if we were to trace a genealogy of positive realism we would not only find Schelling (and the whole of Christian philosophy related to the theme of revelation), but also a tradition in which revelation is far from religious, referring to the fact that the world is given. In this perspective, we also find the origin of thought as emerging from reality. So, to clarify the position of positive realism by means of formulas, we should notice what follows.

Metaphysical realism (if we grant that such a position ever really existed as it is represented by antirealists) supposes a full mirroring of thought and reality:

(1) Thought < - > Reality

Constructivism, finding this relation between two distinct realities incomprehensible, suggests a constitutive role of thought with respect to reality:

(2) Thought > Reality

Positive realism, instead, sees thought as an emerging datum of reality, just like gravity, photosynthesis and digestion.

(3) Thought < Reality

This is why sense 'is given': it is not at our complete disposal, just like the possibilities and impossibilities of the screwdriver. Sense is a mode of organization for which something presents itself in some way. This, however, does not depend on the subjects: it is not the production of some transcendental self with its categories. Here there is rather something like Husserl's passive synthesis or the 'synopsis of sense' enigmatically mentioned by Kant in the first edition of the *Critique of Pure Reason*[16]: The world has its own order before the subject appears. There is something on the background that can become a figure. Thus, we need to show how thought emerges from being. Thanks to Darwin, this process can be conceived of as the development of an (intelligent) epistemology on the basis of a non-intelligent ontology.[17] It is not necessary to think of a spirit determining the passage from ontology to epistemology. One can very well propose an 'upward' perspective, for which the organic is the outcome of the inorganic, conscience emerges from non-conscious elements and epistemology emerges from ontology.[18]

At this point, we have everything we need for a fully articulated system. There is a first level – that of an ontology of the natural world – where the inorganic becomes organic and, eventually, conscious. Then begins a second level: the construction of the social world, in which the role of epistemology is not simply reconstructive, but constructive. This double articulation overturns the setting of negative philosophy: sense is produced by non-sense, possibilities arise from the clash against reality, and philosophy does not have to become a fragmentary view that gives up finding a comprehensive sense to the real. The mind emerges from the world, and in particular from that piece of world that regards it the most: the body and the brain. Then it faces the environment (both natural and social) and itself. In this encounter – which is a reconstruction and a revelation, but not a construction – the mind elaborates (both individually and collectively) an epistemology that takes being as its object. The successful encounter between mind and world, like that between ontology and epistemology, is not guaranteed – error is always possible. But when the mind manages to find accord with the world it comes from (which, I repeat, does not at all amount to providing an exact photograph, also because the world is in perennial motion and is hard to picture), then we have truth.

5. Teleology.

One might bring Thomas Nagel's view as an objection. The scholar, in fact, has recently claimed that the debate between Darwinians and supporters of the 'intelligent plan' has not proved the latter right, but rather shown the former's weakness – in fact, Darwin's hypothesis cannot explain phenomena like conscience, knowledge and values.[19] Indeed, what is the advantage of having a conscience that, as Hamlet put it, 'does make cowards of us'? And how can we explain the emergence of intelligence out of mere matter? As I said, in Darwinian terms one can claim that – just like life is composed of inorganic elements, to which it shall return, in a non-miraculous way – intelligence can very well (or rather, necessarily must) arise from non-intelligent elements. All the same, Nagel sees this conception as a reductionist bias that seems all the more evident when consciousness and intelligence reach very high levels of abstraction, which seem to exclude the very necessity of a mankind capable of thought. As he wrote in 1974: "after all, there would have been transfinite numbers even if everyone had been wiped out by the Black Death before Cantor discovered them."[20] Now, what would the evolutional advantage of transfinite numbers be?

A neo-Darwinian like Stephen Jay Gloud would have claimed that it is a collateral effect of a more developed central nervous system (which is an evolutional advantage *per se*). Nagel, instead, asserts that this is one of the many aspects of the world that Darwinism cannot explain. Nagel's real objective though is not to criticize Darwinism but rather, in positive, to propose the right and ambitious idea of a vaster science, almost a reborn speculative knowledge *à la* German idealism. The fundamental trait of this enlarged science consists in resorting not only to causal explanations (A causes B) but also to final explanations – it is what, in philosophical jargon, is called 'teleology': A causes B because B's purpose was C. For instance, Man developed a cerebral mass superior to that of other primates because s/he was part of a finalised project, whose end was to produce a consciousness. As Dante, a great supporter of teleology, put it: "you were not made to live as brutes, but to pursue virtue and knowledge".

Nagel refers to Aristotle in his claim, but his real predecessor is rather Leibniz in the *Discourse of Metaphysics* (1686): in it, the philosopher is critical of the 'nouveaux philosophes" of his time, who wanted to ban final causes from physics. According to Leibniz[21],a physicist who wished to explain nature only through efficient causes would be limited no less than a historian who tried to explain the conquest of a stronghold without taking into account the objectives of the general who led the battle, merely saying that the particles of powder in the cannon managed to push a hard solid body against the walls of the place, so that it crumbled down. Now, as for the exigency of a teleological science, we could note that natural science (and not only social science, where the recourse to final causes is ever-present) is intrinsically teleological, *without nature being itself teleological*. Kant, in his *Critique of Judgment*, saw this very clearly: when we observe nature through the lens of a scientist, we consider it as a whole and hypothesise its ends. Epistemology, namely what we know or believe to know, is intrinsically teleological: if they show us the section of an eye we won't manage to understand much until we hypothesise that the eye is made for seeing; then the function of the pupil, the crystalline lens and the retina will become clear. But ontology, what there is, is not necessarily teleo-logical. It is so in the social world, not in the natural world that Darwin refers to.

Saying that 'the purpose of the eye is to see', which helps us understand its functioning is just like saying that 'the objective of the two teams is to score' allows us to understand a football match. But this does not force us to claim that the eye was intrin-sically created to see any more than it authorises us to say that the nose was created to support the weight of glasses. It could be an evolutional chance. In such a long time as that separating us from the Big Bang and with such a vast material as the universe, anything can happen, including consciousness and transfinite numbers. This is analogous to the library of Babel imagined by José Luis Borges, which contains everything, including the day and exact time of our death – only, this piece of information (of uncertain evolutional usefulness) is buried between billions of other likely or unlikely hours and days, and billions of billions of meaningless books.

2

Resistance

1. Concepts.

So, we have to start from being, not from knowledge. In order to do so, positive realism turns back to perception (it is no chance that anti-realism always starts from a criticism to perception). Careful: I am not saying that reality amounts to perceptual experience. The path from *aisthesis* to realism is more complex than that, and touches a few points that are central to the whole of modern philosophy – so much so that they tend to come back chronically, like a recidivist.

First of all, it is important to understand why in the twentieth century (especially in the second half) perception appeared to be so little relevant to philosophy. The answer is simple: the great questions were those related to language. In the age of the 'linguistic turn' it didn't make sense to deal with something that, at most, looked like a secondary aspect to be tackled by science – perhaps a second order science like psychology, as philosophers traditionally regard it. It was the age in which it was believed that, as Gadamer put it, "being that can be understood is language"[22] or that, in Derrida's words, "there is nothing outside the text."[23] Things were not different among analytic philosophers, where Davidson argued that we do not encounter perceptions, but beliefs,[24] and Goodman posited that one constructs the world just like one constructs an artwork.[25] The so-called linguistic turn, therefore, was more properly a conceptual turn. What we are and the way in which we live was considered to be a matter of history, language, traditions and texts. And even what was 'out there' in the world of nature is not what we get from the senses, which are always deceitful, but rather what is tackled by the great conceptual constructions through which

11

scientists give shape to the world.

Usually when a philosopher does not have a theory of perception or seems not to worry about it, it means s/he actually has one, but a bad one – most times it consists in claiming that perceptuality is dominated by conceptuality, at least in the Kantian sense that intuitions without concepts are blind. Then the theory widens with examples, showing how perception is determined by culture, expectations, habits, practical ends and the unconscious, which, after all, is also structured like a language. A philosopher who doesn't engage with perception thinks that perception has nothing philosophical about it, ascribing too much importance to concepts in the construction of experience[26] (and not, mind you, in the *re*construction of experience, in the scientific or philosophical description of it, as it would be entirely reasonable to posit).

2. Perception.

What these attitudes presuppose, so as to justify the supposed superiority of the conceptual over the perceptual, is a sort of trick by which perception is expelled from the realm of philosophy by simply exaggerating its shortcomings as a source of knowledge. A classic example of this treatment can be found at the beginning of Hegel's *Phenomenology of Spirit*[27], where we see the condemnation of sensible certainty by way of the condemnation of the 'this'. The passage is well known: sensible certainty tells us that 'now it is day'; Hegel asks us to write this truth down. Twelve hours later, however, this truth is out of date because in the meantime night has arrived. The trick is fairly transparent, but it works pretty well. We start by thinking of perception as a source of knowledge, then we notice that this source is sometimes misleading, and we draw the conclusion that we must withdraw all credibility from perception and look for certainty elsewhere. The aim of disqualifying perception has the significant philosophical advantage of giving a huge boost to the realm of the conceptual, which is then given the task of saving the truth from the illusions and tricks of the senses.

This is even easier to see in Descartes.[28] He begins by claiming that our knowledge comes from the senses, but they sometimes mislead us, and it is better not to trust anything that has deceived us even just once. To the objection that we are deceived only about things that are small or far away, Descartes replies that not only are there madmen who believe they are dressed in purple robes when they are in fact naked, but also that every night we dream and hence what we perceive could be a mere representation. Here, the philosopher's unfairness to the senses is at least threefold. First of all, he emits a radical sentence of condemnation in response to an occasional shortcoming: *sometimes* the senses mislead, therefore we must be *systematically* wary of them. Second, he supposes that the senses should be regarded as genuine bearers of knowledge, in that they bear 'witness'. Finally, he thinks he can establish a radical scepticism by assuming a perfect equivalence between waking life and the dream state, which is clearly not the case – to put it as John Austin, "And what about dreams? Does the dreamer see illusions? Does he have delusions? Neither; dreams are *dreams*."[29]

Hegel and, before him, Descartes thus claim that all knowledge begins with the senses, but then hasten to show the unreliability of the knowledge deriving from them. This is a typical starting point, which we also find in the first lines of the *Critique of Pure Reason*.[30] It is also what Hume does quite explicitly[31]: his assumption is that knowledge comes from sensible experience and is based on inductive reasoning. But then, once he has shown that inductive reasoning is not one hundred percent certain, he draws the sceptical conclusion from it.

I repeat the central point here: the clearest fact about these strategies is that they *give an essentially epistemological role to the senses*, as if they were above all vehicles of knowledge, and then, having pointed out that sensible knowledge does not guarantee certainty, they withdraw all interest from sensibility. They pass from occasional doubt to global doubt. This is where constructivism comes from: from the need to found, by way of construction, a world that has lost its stability and, to put it as Hamlet did, is out of joint".[32] The result, however, is the opposite of what was expected, and is summed up in Price's sentence quoted ironically by Austin: "When I see a tomato, there is much that I *can doubt*".[33]

3. Deconstruction.

The outcome of this unfair trick played on perception was twofold. On the one hand, experience was taken to be magmatic – that is, it was assumed that there were no regularities or necessities in nature, assimilating sensible impressions to the representations of imagination. On the other hand, the power of concepts was made greater and boundless, as it was called to give order to an inconsistent and chaotic matter. Kantian philosophy has become the philosophical mainstream of the last two centuries because it was able to solve the sceptical impasse as it was defined by Hume's critique of induction.[34] Knowledge begins in the senses, but it is such only because it is fixated by a priori conceptual schemes that are independent from sensual experience. As a consequence, "intuitions without concepts are blind"[35] – that is, ontology collapses into epistemology. It is in this framework that we can explain the linguistic turn, i.e. the thesis that being, language and truth are closely connected.

Now, if perception is so easy to disqualify from the epistemological point of view, why is it such a powerful argument for realism? Why does it have such a strong deconstructive power? The answer, at first approximation, is very simple: it is easy to disqualify perception from the epistemological point of view only because it is not treated as perception, but as representation. Under the umbrella-word 'representation' things like seeing a mirage, a hallucination, a dream or an afterimage are completely assimilated to perception, and obviously perception is degraded to pure illusion as a consequence.

For this game to work, two elements are needed. The first is, so to speak, a sort of phenomenological negligence. You would have to be very gullible indeed to mistake a greenish afterimage for a patch on the wall; of course it can happen, but it usually never does. The grain of what is perceived is much finer than that of what is merely thought of, recalled or represented. A remembered fire does not burn; a remembered duck-rabbit does not shift; comparing two remembered colours is always problematic because the real shades have a finer grain than the memory of them. If this is how things are, then the problem merely consisted in assimilating, under the name 'representation', things that are in fact very diverse, only to draw the conclusion that the control of representations derives from conceptual schemes, in line with the constructionism I mentioned a while ago.

The second element is what psychologists call the 'stimulus error', by which they mean the ease with which we replace an observation with an explanation. In other words, it is the ease with which, when we have our eyes closed, we reply 'nothing' or 'blackness' to the question 'what do you see?', when what we see are really phosphenes and flashes. We do not include those in our description because we are talking about something else, namely a theory of vision for which the eye is like a *camera obscura*, so that when the shutter is closed there is total darkness. It is not difficult to find a trace of the stimulus error in the incommensurability of paradigms initially defended by Kuhn[36] – this idea, if followed through, would lead to state that Ptolemy and Copernicus did not have the same perceptual experience of the sun. From this point of view, the very contraposition between manifest image and real image of the world can be traced back to the stimulus error. Thus we can realise that the fundamental way in which this error works is by confusing ontology and epistemology. Besides, in the case of social objects[37], it is hard to find a distinction between manifest image and real image: in a fine or a wedding they actually seem to coincide.

The inherently deconstructive role of perception, ultimately, is this: rather than a source of information and an epistemological resource, it should be considered as a stumbling block to set against our constructivist expectations. In a way, perceptual deconstruction is comparable to falsification in Popper[38], except that here it has an ontological function and not, as in Popper, an epistemological one. It is at this point that we find the importance of perception as well as the ontological meaning of aesthetics as *aisthesis*: the senses sometimes disproof our theories. This is the decisive reason for the philosophical importance of sensibility: it does not passively confirm our expectations and knowledge. On the contrary, it often opposes them, clearly revealing that there is something distinct and separate from us. What emerges from perceptual deconstruction is a 'naive physics'[39] or a 'second naïveté'[40]: the world presents itself to us as real without necessarily claiming on that account to be scientifically true. As I understand it, the appeal to simplicity is not a way to simplify, but to sophisticate our relationship with reality. This is where one draws the dialectic that leads from unamendability to affirmativity.

4. Unamendability.[41]

Sensibility resists conceptuality: it cannot be amended. Now, the unamendable datum that comes from sensibility may even be an error, a delusion, or nonsense, but it certainly *is* something. Unamendability leads us back to the notion of nonconceptual content that was much discussed in the past few decades.[42] It is a contrastive principle, which manifests the real as non-I. It concerns the sphere of experience that lies outside of that of concepts, defining an external world extraneous to knowledge. Nonconceptual content is a resistance, something that cannot be nullified. At the same time, it is also an autonomous organisation of experience, which reduces the burden of the ordering activity that is attributed to conceptual schemes. In fact, the activity of conceptual schemes applies primarily to knowledge, but it seems excessive to also attribute to them the organization of ordinary experience, as is done by the philosophies of the Kantian-hermeneutic matrix. Moreover, there is also a sense in which conceptual thought may not lie in the head – as, for example, when I make calculations with pen and paper or with an abacus. Everything is outside, inside I have nothing, and yet it seems that I am calculating.[43]

5. Affirmativity.

Finally, let's come to affirmativity. The dialectic of positive realism is able to explain how positivity can emerge out of negativity. It is not a miraculous transmutation, but simply the use of resources inherent in the real world, which is able to support and invite precisely insofar as it is able to resist. For instance, there was an age in which the whole of mankind supported geocentrism. In that age, geocentrism depended on the subjects and their (supposed) knowledge, but the fact remains that the epistemologically true theory – i.e. heliocentrism – was independent of the subjects. Heliocentrism depends on a state of things, namely the fact that the Earth revolves around the Sun. In other words, heliocentrism is stronger than geocentrism because it doesn't depend on the subjects. Ultimately, this affirmativity of the real constitutes the unsurpassable limit to any constructivist hyperbole, and this limit is the greatest merit of perception. It is in this sense that what exists, ontology, is first and foremost what resists.

This ontological character of being, in my opinion, is constitutive; it is in this sense that my perspective differs from the view brilliantly defended by Markus Gabriel[44], for whom "to exist is to appear in a field of sense". Gabriel's theory means, for instance, that Harry Potter exists in the field of meaning of fantastic literature and atoms exist in that of physics. The only thing that, for Gabriel, does not exist is the world, understood not as the physical universe, but as the sum of all fields of sense: the field of sense of all fields of sense (i.e. the absolute) does not exist. Nevertheless, making ontology depend on a field of sense – that is, if not on epistemology at least on something tied to subjectivity – reproposes a version, although a weakened one, of the transcendental fallacy. Furthermore, it leaves open the problem of nonhuman beings, of those we call (in such a confused manner) 'animals': it is hard to claim that there is, for them, a field of sense in which there are atoms or characters like Harry Potter. But it is problematic (also from a moral point of view) to exclude the existence, for instance, of death in a slaughterhouse – which, nonetheless, can be hardly inserted (both for an animal and for a human) into a 'field of sense', since it presents itself as an opaque and resisting nonsense.

So, the moral of what I have said so far is the following: to exist is to resist. This motto should be understood in two ways. The first is openly political, but I won't spend much time on it as I have already tackled it elsewhere.[45] I will merely say here that considering reality as something docile and malleable can justify any kind of mystification. The second way is ontological. Quine said that "to be is to be the value of a bound variable"[46] and that "there is no entity without identity"[47] – these sayings imply the absorption of ontology into epistemology, and postulate that being is transparent so that only what is clear and distinct exists. Well, to this I object that being as resistance is a concrete noumenon, a multiplicity of things-in-themselves that constitutes the ordinary furniture of our experience, as well as the possibility of the world both for us humans and for beings with conceptual schemes and perceptual apparatuses different from ours.

3

Objects

1. Phenomena?

The affirmativity of objects manifests the richness of the non-I: "being is said in many ways".[48] This saying was often considered the justification of a generic pluralism, an ontological 'anything goes', while it is the premise of a theory of the object as the foundation of ontology. One of the most persistent consequences of transcendentalism – understood as the systematic prevalence of epistemology over ontology – is the fact that it makes no sense to speak of objects, since they are but the outcome of a cognitive strategy, phenomena obeying to categories (Kant), or even mere appearances produced by the principle of reason that shapes the world (Schopenhauer). The thesis I wish to defend[50] is therefore that – recalling Aristotle's metaphysics, Meinong's theory of objects[51], last century's American 'new realism'[52], and contemporary 'object-oriented philosophy'[53] – we should start from objects (an area in which, as I said, subjects are also included), so as to reduce the gap between our theories and our experience of the world.

In fact, for at least the past two centuries, we have been suffering from an exotropic strabismus as regards objects. With one eye, that of common sense, we are convinced to be surrounded by things that are exactly what they are: tables, chairs, computers. These things rarely turn out to be different from what they look like, or to be illusions or mirages. These are only fleeting moments: things do not usually deceive and, for certain, they deceive less than people do. But there is a second eye with which we look at the world, one that is more exigent and philosophical and sees things in an entirely different way. For it, we deal not with things but with phenomena that are the

19

outcome of the encounter between an inaccessible thing-in-itself – the object we are referring to – and the mediation offered by our perceptive apparatuses and conceptual schemes.

The thinker that most of all tied his name to this transformation is Kant, who based much of his theory of phenomena on secondary qualities (like colours).[54] When I turn on the light the table is white, but if I turn it off the table is black, or at least I cannot see it. How can I say that the table is a thing-in-itself? Evidently, it depends on me, whereas primary qualities such as extension and impenetrability do not. Kant, however, extends this circumstance to primary qualities, which in the transcendental perspective are subordinate to space and time, as they are pure forms of sensibility placed in us and not in the world. Yet, seducing as it may be from a theoretical point of view, this theory generates a large number of problems.

The first problem is that of the location of phenomena. Kant asserts, for example, that the colour red is not an attribute of a rose (this topic is closely related to the argument on colours that disappear when the light is off).[55] At this point, however, some difficult questions must be answered. If the redness is not in the rose, then where is it? In our minds? Somewhere in between? And if it is in fact in our minds, then why is it not blue or any other colour? We must not forget that the only glimpse of the thing-in-itself in the Kantian *corpus* concerns this very redness[56]: it is when Kant (entirely contradicting the transcendental perspective) states that if cinnabar were not permanently red our imagination would never be able to associate to the colour red other properties of the mineral, such as its weight and shape.

The second problem is the 'nesting of phenomena'. It develops an argument originally brought forward by Strawson[57], who noted how spatial phenomena, being contained within temporal phenomena, are phenomena to the second power. Nonetheless, we can observe that, since temporal phenomena are in turn contained within the I think, which in turn is a phenomenon, then spatial phenomena become phenomena to the third power. And there is nothing to prevent an infinite progress or regress, in which case we would have phenomena of phenomena of phenomena.

The third and final problem concerns, so to speak, authenticity. If we consider that Kant includes the I think (that is, ourselves as well as all other human beings) among phenomena, then at least three problems arise. First, when I feel pain I would have to think of it as a pure phenomenon, an appearance, and not as a thing-in-itself and an irreducible qualitative element. Second, I could be completely different from what I believe to be, in which case punishment or reward, just like the entire moral world, would no longer have any value — Kant suggested this when he asserted that, in the world of phenomena, we have no proof of the fact that there has ever been, in the history of the world, a single free action. Third, we would find ourselves considering ourselves, along with our friends and relatives, as phenomena (while we usually consider them as things-in-themselves), leading to odd propositions such as 'my daughter is a phenomenon and not a thing-in-itself'. Normal elements of grammar of relations, the meaning of our ipseity and of the first-person character of our experiences, the otherness of our neighbour: all this would disappear and, in particular, we would be unable to explain the reason why feeling extraneous to oneself (which should be the physiology of an I think recognised as a phenomenon) is normally perceived as a pathology.

If we consider these difficulties, then perhaps we are entitled to a real Copernican revolution, one that would put the subject at the margins, and not at the centre, of experience. And we might realise that things-in-themselves are all but rare; in fact, they make up a rather lush jungle, constituting the fabric of our material, social and ideal word. Let us verify this.

2. Natural Objects.

Natural objects. Let us begin with natural objects. For Kant, they are the phenomena *par excellence*: they are situated in space and time, and yet they are not to be found in nature. They are in our heads, along with the categories we use to give order to the world, to the point that, without human beings, space and time may disappear as well. We should conclude that, before mankind, there were no objects, or at least not as we know them. Yet it clearly is not so: fossils prove that there were beings that existed before any human being: before Kant, before Berkeley, before Descartes and any 'I think' in general. If they existed before us, they were things-in-themselves and not phenomena (i.e. things that appear *to us*). So how do we deal with this?

Obviously, one could object that the minute we look at them, now, they turn into phenomena. But let us hypothesise that the fossil is accidentally found by a dog. The dog has conceptual schemes and perceptive apparatuses radically different from our own, and yet he manages to interact with fossils (and with a number of more recent objects, like non-prehistoric bones) just like we do. So, is there any good reason to believe that there are two objects, the fossil seen by the dog and the fossil seen by us? And if there is only one object, why should it not be a thing-in-itself? This interaction cannot be explained unless we admit that the dog is dealing with the thing-in-itself – otherwise it would be a case of miraculous harmony between different phenomena. Thus, the argument of the fossil (i.e. pre-existence) is entangled with that of interaction (which I have illustrated elsewhere with the slipper experiment[58], showing that beings endowed with radically different conceptual schemes and perceptual apparatuses do interact with the same things-in-themselves).

3. Artefacts.

Of course, this does not only hold for natural objects, but also for artefacts (slippers, tables, chairs and supermarket objects) that are for us the quintessence of objects. Of course, they depend on us for their fabrication. But, once fabricated, they can be used by beings with conceptual schemes and perceptual apparatuses radically different from our own. Our cat is perfectly able to curl up on our sofa. Why think that the sofa is one thing for us and another for her? What prevents us from thinking that the sofa (but also cat-food, for that matter) are things-in-themselves?

Everything I've said about the 'invite' of the world presupposes that objects have the initiative. This is particularly visible in artefacts as, in them, the invite is a fundamental part of the object itself (the chair invites to sit, the handle to be handled and so forth). Artefacts were made with a purpose, but this does not mean that they can only be used for their original goal. Computers have evolved independently from our original previsions: a calculation tool turned into a multimedia machine. And this is just one of the infinite examples of the fact that objects evolve based on their inherent invite characters, much more than they do following the subject's plans. Rather, the subjects accept the objects' invite and act accordingly.

4. Social objects.

Upon closer inspection, it becomes clear that social objects, which depend on subjects (while not being subjective), are also things-in-themselves and not phenomena. This may seem complicated at first because, if social objects depend on conceptual schemes, then it should obviously follow that they are phenomena. But it is not so. In order to be a phenomenon, it is not enough to depend on conceptual schemes. A phenomenon must also be in contrast with things-in-themselves. Now, there is a universe of things like marriages and divorces, financial crises, banknotes and academic titles, and it would be quite difficult to argue that these are simple phenomena, or masks of a Thing-In-Itself that loves to hide. Let us consider a fine. What would be its 'in-itself'? To say that a fine is an apparent fine is to simply say that it is not a fine; a true fine is a thing-in-itself, just like a real 10-euro banknote, a will or a vehicle registration form.

In the case of social objects we have a perfect coincidence of internal and external, as is demonstrated by the fact that the disappearance of appearance involves the disappearance of essence. What kind of wedding is one that everyone forgets about (including those directly involved) and whose documents are lost? Weddings, tribunals and altars are systematically accompanied by memory, and by the technological prosthesis of memory constituted by writing. It is no chance that writing (even though its end was prophesised not long ago) is the centre of the greatest revolution of our age: the revolution of emails, tablets, phones that turned into writing machines, and everything being recorded on some 'writing surface'' or another. Writing can never die, because it is indispensable to the construction of social reality: think of the billions of people who died remaining forever unknown, because writing had not been invented yet. The names of biblical patriarch and Egyptian pharaohs, though, we still know today.

5. Ideal Objects.
Now consider ideal objects. Is $2 + 2 = 4$ a phenomenon? Perhaps. But only provided that a Cartesian daemon pretends that $2 + 2 = 4$, while in reality $2 + 2 = 5$. Aside from this consideration, all objects of thought, even in strictly Kantian terms, are things-in-themselves, given that Kant expressly asserts that he established the distinction between phenomenon and noumenon in order to limit sensibility's claims of access to things-in-themselves. Since ideal objects are outside space and time independently from the subjects, there should be no reason to state that they are phenomena and not things-in-themselves, given that one of their main characters is that they develop their properties independently of the subjects' will.

6. Feelings.

Furthermore, once the contradictions of the Self and the Other as phenomena examined above have been taken into consideration, who could deny that feelings are things-in-themselves? If I state that I am happy, could anyone object that I am so only as a phenomenon, and that perhaps as something-in-itself I am sad? As a matter of fact, the distinction between euphoria and happiness or between depression and sadness exists, proving that feelings such as happiness and sadness are things-in-themselves, and are also tied to other things-in-themselves; that is, the existence of objects outside us that cause happiness or sadness (as opposed to what occurs in euphoria or depression).

Feelings are often related to events, things like hurricanes or car accidents. Which are often unpredictable. Irregularity and surprise (i.e. the world disregarding our data and expectations) are the clearest demonstration of the fact that the world is much more extensive and unpredictable than our conceptual schemes. Beware: being realists does not amount to being pessimists, as a surprise may very well be pleasant. I would like to conclude this section with a hedonistic thought: the world of phenomena is boring and predictable, but the world of things-in-themselves holds some surprises – even pleasant ones.

4

Realisms

1. Internal.

Surprises make us change our mind, and to change one's mind, in philosophy, is both possible and necessary – even somehow dutiful. What matters is what one changes one's mind about. If we read Hilary Putnam's *Philosophy in an Age of Science*,[59] we will realize that Putnam has certainly not changed his mind on science, which remains the lodestar of his thought. At a closer look, he has not changed his mind on realism either, as it has always been present in his philosophical agenda. What Putnam did change his mind about is perception, and he did so in a clamorous and significant way, because it led him to formulate a theory of direct perception (that is, the independence of perception from concepts), which implies a radical transformation in relation to the Kantian horizon in which Putnam had initially started.

In *Realism with a Human Face* (1990), at the end of the age of internal realism, Putnam still claimed that elements like language and mind penetrate so deeply into what we call 'reality' (a term that Putnam, in accordance with the dominant spirit of the time, wrote between inverted commas), that any plan to represent ourselves as mapping something independently from language is compromised to begin with. Much water has passed under the bridge since then, and in *Philosophy in an Age of Science* Putnam announces a forthcoming book on perception written with Hilla Jacobson, committing to a deep criticism of John McDowell. In fact, in *Mind and World*, the latter restated a Kantian-analytical creed for which language, conceptual schemes and in general our 'second nature' intervene so deeply in our perception that it necessarily acquires a conceptual character.[60] In an even more

27

recent work, Putnam pushed himself to an apodictic statement: "if we cannot explain how perception allows us to understand reality, every description of realism will be forever incomplete".[61]

2. Scientific.

The point is clear: it already was when Putnam added the third party *body* to McDowell's 'mind' and 'world' hendiadys. The crucial problem with internal realism is that its general approach is the same as McDowell's: predominance of conceptual schemes also at a perceptive level or, in other words, undisputed dominion of the conceptual over the real. I realise that an equivalence between 'perceptive' and 'real' – as posited by the theories of direct perception – needs an explanation; I will clarify this later, for now I shall try to explicate it in Putnam's terms. For him, the real problem was to speak of 'internal realism': he should have spoken instead of 'scientific realism'.[62] Now, what is the difference?

There is a great difference indeed. To say 'scientific realism' means laying one's cards on the table while supporting a fully sharable thesis: there is no science without conceptual schemes, and, obviously, the reality grasped by science is intrinsically outlined by concepts. Science talks about viruses, serotonin and bosons, namely things we have no direct experience of. This, of course, does not mean that these things are the product of the scientists' theories. With regard to this, Putnam also confesses to regretting a sentence like "the mind and the world jointly make up the mind and the world", adding a little later that confusing the construction of the *notion* of "boson' (a theory) with the construction of *real* quantum systems (a reality) is a form of idealism.[63]

Well, this was precisely the problem with middle Putnam's 'internal realism'. Speaking of 'internal realism' instead of 'scientific realism' means falling into what I have called 'transcendental fallacy' – the belief that conceptual schemes, through which we approach the real, are not the forms of a (more or less refined) scientific knowledge, but rather the prerequisite of any experience of the world, also by those who know absolutely nothing about science. This is why a thesis like 'intuitions without concepts are blind', which is so suitable for describing the proceedings of scientific research, results so inappropriately for describing our ordinary experience, where conceptualisation plays a more than marginal role. In particular, it is radically inadequate for describing perception, which is essentially characterised by its stubborn independence from concepts.

As Gaetano Kanizsa wrote, "the eye, if we really want it to think, still thinks in its own way".[64] If we also add that one of the most shared outcomes of psychology of thought is that our own everyday reasoning is not marked by some form of scientific rationality, then it seems quite evident that the identification between experience and science proposed by internal realism is no less than problematic. We might even go a little further and claim that the difference between science and experience is the 'subjective' reflection, so to speak, of a radical distinction that takes place in reality: that between epistemology and ontology. Which is precisely the difference that internal realism erases, so that what there is, is identified with the knowledge we have of it.

3. Transcendental.

Kant had also noticed the problems with 'internal realism' but, unlike Putnam, he never admitted to changing his mind. And if historians distinguish between a precritical Kant and a transcendentalist Kant, more or less after 1770, no one, at least that I know of, noted that between the *Critique of Pure Reason* and the *Critique of Judgment* Kant changed his mind no less drastically than Putnam did between *Reason, Truth and History* and *Mind, Body and World*.[65] The *Critique of Pure Reason*, in fact, can be regarded as the archetype of every form of internal realism.

In what we could define as 'transcendental realism', we have no contact with the external world, but only with a world internal to our conceptual schemes. It seems that Kant thought of himself as a realist while being an idealist, not only judging from the immediate outcomes of Kantism, but also because the Copernican revolution consists in claiming that 'the mind and the world jointly make up the mind and the world'. Notwithstanding this, Kant still wanted to be a realist (otherwise he would not have opposed scepticism) and, worrying about being interpreted in an idealistic sense, he modified the *Critique of Pure Reason* in its second edition by inserting a simply more opaque Transcendental Deduction, a confutation of idealism that could not be more idealistic, and most of all a chapter on schematism: namely the bit committed to explaining how concepts can construct experience.

Next to these (far from decisive) changes, though, Kant makes two important moves which have been underestimated. The first is the publication, in 1786, of the *Metaphysical Foundations of Natural Science*, in which he transposes the system of principles that, in the *Critique of Pure Reason*, was meant to shape our experience, presenting those principles as the rules presiding over the functioning of science. That is, he silently passes from 'internal realism' to 'scientific realism'. A few years later, with the *Critique of Judgment*, he makes another, even more important, move by presenting the book as the accomplishment of his critical system. But it was not at all so: it was a complete break with the past.

First of all, in the critique of aesthetic judgment, Kant writes that the beautiful pleases without a concept: in other words, he dethrones the conceptual, and does so in a sphere where the perceptive is particularly important. Secondly, in the critique of teleological judgment, Kant explicitly proposes a theory of science: nature has no end in itself, it is we who assign ends to it in order to investigate it scientifically. Thirdly, although Kant claims that the reflective judgment (which, introduced in the

Third Critique, retraces the rule from the single instances) has to
be set next to the determining judgment of the First Critique
(which from the rule descends to the single instances) there are
very good reasons to believe that, rather than integration, it is a
matter of replacement. In fact, it is hard to see how the determining judgment could coexist with the reflective judgment in a
strange amphibious modality in which it would be up to the
subject to chose which one to use. In any case, the subject, if
willing to use the reflective judgment (and we can be sure he
would only use that one), would not be able to respond to
Hume's objections, because in fact the reflective judgment is, to
all intents and purposes, empirical induction, which indeed
retraces the rule from the single instances.

4. External.

Once it is clear that conceptual schemes regulate science but not
experience, perception – namely the function that allows for our
contact with the external world – comes back into play. By
'external world" I mean a *world external to our conceptual
schemes*.[66] Here it is necessary to make a clarification. Due to a
curious misunderstanding, what I propose to call 'external
realism' is sometimes mistaken for 'metaphysical realism', the
old and obviously false idea that the mind reflects the world and
philosophy is 'the mirror of nature', which is absurd: mirrors
reflect with no effort, while philosophy and science work inten-
sively in order to know reality. External realism – which, I
believe, Putnam could also adopt now – is not a form of
metaphysical realism, but rather a criticism of internal realism.
Its reference to perception means appealing to its negativity, to
its saying 'no' to conceptual schemes and to its disappointing our
expectations. Those who claim that we never have a relationship
with the world but only with our thought postulate a surreal and
incredible harmony, for at least two reasons.

First of all, for the benefit of possible objectors – such as

Gentile, who affirms that reality is not thinkable if not in relation to the thinking activity, hence claiming that even when I am suffering from a rheumatism I am actually just thinking it – I would suggest to consider what follows. I might very well think that when I stare at the screen and the keyboard I am typing on, it is me thinking of the screen and the keyboard. Yet, this does not entail that I have a relation with the screen and keyboard only when I think. The resistance that my body feels in this very moment in being sat on the chair does not only exist in my thought nor is it only known through it. The part of my body on which I sit was never considered a place of thought, not even by the most fervent idealists. Moreover, the computer – which I see with my eyes and think about with my brain – is still a being represented as external, not internal. And so every possible pain in the part of my body on which I sit would be felt as a pain in *that* part of the body and not as a headache – as should probably be expected if we only had a relationship with our thought.

Furthermore, if perception truly were a docile colony for conceptual schemes, it would be much more easily influenced by thought than it actually is. It is, in fact, perception and not thought (which turns out to be much more accommodating, especially if combined with imagination) that gives us the rough feeling that something out there exists, and it does so by notifying us that what exists first of all resists, says "no", refusing to be colonised by thought. Perception is therefore far from being a privileged tool of knowledge (there is undoubtedly better stuff on the market), but it is rather a repertoire of frustrations, or at least disappointments – of things being in a way that cannot be changed.

5. Positive.

The reference to perception, though, is not simply an appeal to negativity, to the resistance of the hard core of reality, impermeable and unamendable. It is also a hint at what I have proposed we call 'positive realism'. In fact, we don't receive from reality only confutations of the pretensions of conceptual schemes: we also get positive indications. Very simply: the chair I am sat on does not only resist my weight, it also supports me, with an affordance (an invite) that might very well hold true also for beings other than myself. This is what my experience is telling me, therefore letting me know not only a negativity, but also a positivity. Moreover, science tells me that the physical components of the chair are such that they can ensure support, which would happen even if I knew nothing about it: this is particularly interesting because it testifies that, in the object (the chair), the encounter between science and commonsense takes place.

This is also Putnam's perspective, as he puts forward (here and elsewhere) the project of conciliating the *positive* components of commonsense with scientific realism, so as to guarantee the existence of both the world of ordinary experience and that of microphysics. This plea to positive realism is an attempt at leading philosophy out of the programmatic anti-realism it found shelter in for the past two centuries. The aim of philosophy is not to create an alternative world to that posited by science, whether through reference to commonsense and the 'world of life' or through the transcendence of commonsense and the search for paradoxes. It is a matter of bridging the divide between science and commonsense, between what we think (or what scientists think) and what we experience.

6. Minimal.

This project of conciliation can be developed with a minimalistic approach, for which there are good pragmatic reasons to posit a complementarity between science and commonsense, and with a maximalist approach, for which the identity of science and commonsense can be enunciated in ontological terms. Putnam has always been a supporter of the first option. In many areas one can do philosophy *without* science, but never *against* science. At most, one can radically do without it, following Putnam's internal realism, which from this perspective, seems extremely close to Rorty's point of view. In fact, we have the proof of the efficiency of science in life itself, and for Putnam realism is the only philosophy that does not turn science's success into a miracle.

With the miracle argument – which Putnam enunciated in 1975 (that is, at the start of his internal realism phase) and which he still defends now, almost forty years later – the burden of proof is given to the anti-realist side. If there were no *one* reality working as a substratum both for the world of life and for that of science, how would we explain the fact that the latter is so efficacious on the first? To a sort of occasionalism? To a pre-established harmony? The problem with this argument is though, that it exposes itself to a counter-objection, because the anti-realist could still reply: "If you cannot give me valid arguments in favour of realism, apart from the functional efficaciousness of science, then this efficaciousness might very well be simply a miracle, and yours an act of faith".

The fact that Putnam is not very sensitive to this possible objection – which he does not even consider in his deep discussion of the criticism to the miracle argument[67] – depends, I believe, on two reasons. The first is that this is not his only argument in favour of realism, but it is rather a specific argument against scientific conventionalism (we can defend realism in other fields of experience, for instance in ethics, without resorting to the miracle argument). The second is that Putnam elaborated this argument when he adopted internal realism. Thanks to the Copernican revolution, our conceptual schemes adapt to a world that they partly constitute, in a world of experience that is absorbed by the world of science. Nonetheless, I believe, once we clarify that instead of 'internal realism' we should speak of 'scientific realism'', this solution is no longer enough for Putnam, as it looks like a sort of miracle itself – or at least like a form of mysterianism, like when Eugene Wigner, winner of the Nobel Prize for physics, spoke of the "unreasonable efficaciousness of mathematics".

7. Speculative.

One should certainly avoid being a realist by faith (albeit a pragmatist and functionalist faith) and not by reason. This holds especially in a field so delicate and essential as the ontological justification of science, which is the basis of its accordance with commonsense: science and experience refer differently to the same world. For this reason, I think it is necessary to abandon Putnam's minimalism. We should try instead a maximalist commitment, that could be called 'speculative' (along the lines of Anglo-French speculative realism)[68] because it shares the ambition of the great speculative systems of the idealistic age: that is, to philosophically account for the integration between science and commonsense. This integration requires two interventions, one on the level of structure, the other on the level of genesis.

On the level of structure – that is, of how relations between science and experience as well as epistemology and ontology give themselves to us – we have to keep the separation of the two levels, so as not to fall into the misunderstandings of constructivism or internal realism. There is no doubt that one thing is what there is and another thing is what we know of what there is. In the same way, there is no doubt that, in the natural world (unlike the social world) what we know does not construct what there is. On the basis of this distinction, we can make a first acquisition: social sciences are efficacious because they apply to the human world a product of the human world itself. For natural sciences the path is undoubtedly longer, but it is still a possible one. It is a matter of finding the ontological foundations of epistemology. And here the genetic level comes into play: it is a matter of accounting for the ontological level that offered the preconditions for the emergence of epistemology (as the specialised second human nature) and commonsense (as generic second human nature).

Obviously, starting from the objects and their opacity involves being aware that a full totality can never be achieved, and that our relationship with the world is a confusing balance between ontology and epistemology.[69] This, however, does not mean that the positivity of these objects is precluded to us. On the contrary, it is this positivity that allows us to be in the world despite the fact that our notions are rarely clear and distinct. Being in the world, at this point, coincides with an attitude that could be summarized by two lines of T.S. Eliot: "Oh, do not ask, 'What is it?'/ Let us go and make our visit".

Fiction

1. Prevalence.

Thus far I have only spoken about aspects regarding the most elementary level of our existence, as if reality had only to do with sense data and mistakes. Obviously, it is not so: reality reaches up to the most abstract forms of human expression. Even the most hermetic poem regurgitates reality (objects, colours, smells, proper names and history), just as the wildest fantasy is entirely made of reality, even if it were merely made of colours. In order not to widen the scope of this section too much, I would like to limit myself to three uses of the real in literature that bear witness to what I would call 'prevalence' of the real.

The first concerns the way in which the real bursts into fiction: I call this mode 'alimentation', because fiction does indeed draw from the real its nutrition and most importantly, as we will see, details and surprises little accessible to imagination. The second is the way in which sometimes the pretext of fiction, i.e. what we might call 'poetic license', is used to mitigate the consequences of one's claims. I call this mode 'denial': the literary work asserts that the facts narrated are imaginary and that the opinions expressed are literary, in order to avoid censorship of various kinds. This mode is particularly interesting because it is the strongest evidence – indirectly, by means of a denial – of the extent to which fiction is steeped in reality. The third, finally, refers to the postmodern world, in which theory itself purported to be literaturised. I call this mode 'derealisation': it is the extension of the mode of denial. Not only are certain statements (otherwise false or morally serious) possible in a literary context, precisely because the context is literary, but they are also possible in a theoretical context – that is, in a discourse that was traditionally considered truthful – because this discourse theorizes the loss of the distinction between reality and fiction, and between philosophy and literature.

These three ways to represent the relationship between fiction and reality are poorly connected, as the thread that unites them is simply the fact that all three of them are represented in the contemporary cultural landscape. The minimalist moral that can be drawn from this is therefore simply that realism – as well as anti-realism – is said in many ways that are not always transparent, and that reality, far from being predictable, is always a step ahead of any fiction.

2. Alimentation.

The first use that fiction makes of the real, then, is that of the real as surprise, the real as alimentation. This is what constitutes the absolute advantage of referring to reality in literature. What Kleist could have imagined the story of the African man who goes around killing people with a pickaxe, which actually happened in Milan? It is a sort of more dramatic Michael Kohlhaas, because the demand for justice that turns into a crime is not even self-aware, and falls upon the innocent. On this whole story prevails the stigma of the real, with its surprise, its unpredictability, its 'sticking out' – as Walter Siti rightly pointed out.[70] In fact, the hallmark of realism lies in denying the Aristotelian principle that a plausible falsehood is better than an implausible truth.

These laws apply in rhetoric and in the administration of evidence in courts, not in literature. But reality overcomes fiction, if only because it is more neat, dry, unpredictable and poetic. This circumstance is the origin of literary realism of all times, and therefore also of the compositions mixing history and invention that fill the contemporary cultural landscape. Think of the judicial materials used by Roberto Saviano in *Gomorrah*, the crowd of strictly historical characters (and of strictly philological recipes) that populates Umberto Eco's *The Prague Cemetery*, or the tacit withdrawals from Wikipedia made by Michel Houellebecq in *The Map and The Territory*. Consumer literature is largely a child of Wikipedia, which, if nothing else, spares us intimism.

Fiction is made on the sofa, so to speak, while reality hits us. Inside the most complicated of all possible worlds (think of sci-fi), most of the elements come from real worlds: in fact, from our own world.[71] Reality is often opposed to possibility, and we see reality as inherently negative, only able to resist and impede us. Well, the real undoubtedly has this feature. At the same time, however, it is also the source of possibility, because it is precisely from what there is that possibilities open up (and in fact possibility is distinguished from mere conceivability).[72] After all, what I am saying is already written in *Aesthetics* by Baumgarten – i.e. a Leibnizian, and therefore a philosopher who was very fond of possibility – who recommended to writers who had run out of topics to consult an 'ontological handbook', a book that contained a classification of objects. Stories hide inside objects. Inside the real, inside what there is, possibility – what that there may be – is so to speak 'embedded'. Each of us is what s/he is, with his/her history and nature, and *because of this* certain possibilities open to him/her, rather than others. Most importantly, it is because many things were realized that many others have simply remained possible.

If this is how things are, then, it becomes particularly difficult to establish what 'realism' is in literature, or, better, to find a radically anti-realist literature. Of course, there is a trivial sense in which *War and Peace* is more realistic than *Alice in Wonderland*, but this distinction is incredibly vague – as you can tell by thinking about Gadda's *Acquainted with Grief* or Proust's *Recherche*. Those novels undoubtedly speak, and very realistically, of their author, but do so in different settings from the geographical or historical reality (neither Maradagal nor Albertine ever existed). Even Abbott's *Flatland*, which takes place in a two-dimensional world, speaks of Victorian society, just as *Gulliver's Travels* tell us about society of the early-eighteenth century, and in a much more realistic way – as it is more raw and unscrupulous thanks to the fantastic setting – than the way in which *Heart* by De Amicis tells us about late-nineteenth century society (suffice it to say that the latter came out in 1886, the year in which Nietzsche published *Beyond Good and Evil*, when indeed the world of Enrico, De Rossi and Garrone had turned into a tale). The game of literature consists precisely in this: it is its specificity.

But if they wrote in newspapers that the mad hatter exists, we would have every right to protest. In fact, we have actually got quite close to that (think of the Gulf war), and not only for the natural human tendency to praise those in power, but also due to a confusion that was typical of postmodernism: namely the doctrine that, since there is as much construction and narrative in literature as in history, there is no difference between history and fiction. Such thesis is not only wrong, as Aristotle had already seen, but also very dangerous because it constitutes *de facto* the justification of any revisionism. But more on this later, when I'll discuss 'derealisation'. For the moment I would just like to clarify that, in my opinion, the appeal to realism does not lie in requiring that the contents of novels should be certified by a committee of historians, but simply in not confusing literature with history, or medicine, or philosophy. Because there is an essential difference (and this is basic common sense) between a novel on the one hand, and a history book, a medical record and a philosophical essay on the other.

3. Denial.

Let us come to denial. Here the appeal to the literary register is used as the justification of claims that would be inadmissible in a 'serious' context. Denial is particularly interesting because it simultaneously affirms and denies its realistic character or, more accurately, according to Freud, it affirms it by denying it. It is, very simply, the classic disclaimer "any resemblance to real persons, living or dead, is purely coincidental". In some cases there are more interesting dynamics, involving, in addition to the author, the professional interpreter. For example Baudelaire in *My Heart Laid Bare* writes as follows: "A pretty conspiracy to organize for the extermination of the Jewish Race./The Jews, Librarians and witnesses of Redemption".[73] Had this been written by a politician, a scientist, a journalist, and maybe even a mediocre poet, it would probably not have been forgiven. Instead, as Derrida pointed out, Benjamin, commenting on the passage, calls it a 'gauloiserie', i.e. a slightly inappropriate joke, while Claude Pichois, the curator of the works of Baudelaire by Gallimard, writes that the passage "is difficult to interpret," but that "any anti-Semitism is to be excluded".

Speaking of Gallimard, Richard Millet (the editor, who also edited a problematic book such as Littell's *The Kindly Ones*) had the idea to write a short Literary Praise for Anders Breivik. He described Breivik's gesture as endowed with aesthetic dignity and formal perfection – only to be surprised by the following reactions. On a smaller scale, there is also the case of *Paradies: Liebe*, the work that the Austrian Ulrich Seidl presented in Venice, in which a religious maniac mistreats her Islamic husband in a wheelchair and even makes love with the crucifix. Albeit in reference to a very different situation, Millet and Seidl were convinced that their representations were legitimate because they fell within the sphere of art.

As in other cases, from Drieu Larochelle to great writers such as Céline or Ezra Pound, one wonders how it is possible that – in a circuit in which everything, even Clint Eastwood's slams, acquire an immediate political relevance – there should be a particular franchise for a practice as visible and media-related as art. This very hypothesis of immunity lead Stockhausen – an author who only shares with Eastwood the fact of being an artist – to state that 9/11 was "the greatest work of art that exists for the whole cosmos". There is a first simple explanation for this, which concerns the inherently fictional nature of art. Everything that is represented, written or described in art, as realistic as its theme and reference may be, is fictional (at least in the intentions declared by the author), so it can be declassified as untrue or not serious. Obviously, problems arise when, as in the case of Millet or Stockhausen, the recipient of the literary praise has made a non-literary killing, or when, as in Nitsch's carnages, the animals slaughtered die for real.

But there is a second explanation, a little longer, which touches on a complicated matter in our culture and explains the use of denial. Unlike other civilizations, ours has developed a sort of 'art religion' characterised by a sacral immunity. This religion is dear to the secular bourgeoisie who, in the nineteenth century found in it an acceptable surrogate for the absolute – this still happens today, as you can tell by the tortures that we are sometimes willing to endure in the name of art. The artists are taken to be extraterritorial and close to delinquents, as Freud noticed, but a certain envy hides behind such judgments. "These artists, you know what they are like," says the audience leaving the theatre or the museum, convinced, however, that what they have seen has made them better by bringing them to another, better world.

After all, it was a great philosopher and a dissatisfied petit bourgeois like Nietzsche that said "l'art pour l'art = to hell with morality". The poet is a seer visited by the gods, he is not responsible for what he says, precisely by the virtue of his inspiration, and on occasion he may be politically incorrect, as he enjoys the franchise of the court jester. In fact, there is another justification for irresponsibility in art that is symmetrical to this one: it regards the poet not as a prophet but as a divine trickster (think of Aldo Palazzeschi's "let me have fun").

So far so good. But even here anti-realism can only go up to a certain point, as reality claims its rights. The fact is, simply, that sometimes what should apparently upset us and drag us out of the constraints of the ordinary, actually touches our deepest, very visceral and trivial chords, like latent xenophobia (as in the case of praise for Breivik). In this case the literary franchise is nothing but the evocation of something removed that would be better kept buried. You can see it well in the futurist machismo, which celebrates the slap, the fist, the war, disrespect for women and the burning of libraries, expressing very ordinary feelings. And this obviously does not end with futurism or with the storms of steel narrated by Jünger. It grows with mass media and culminates in the internet, which is full of poetic licenses indeed: it can happen that even a blogger or a tweeter would claim to have literary immunity – especially if it is a literate speaking of other literates, as in the case of the *post mortem* attacks by Bret Easton Ellis on David Foster Wallace.

Now, this aesthetic immunity is not neutral. Benjamin had seen this very well in *The Work of Art in the Age of Mechanical Reproduction*: the seemingly unpolitical gesture of the aestheticisation of war and evil is actually hyper-political, and its message is 'fiat ars – pereat mundus'. Better then to lay one's cards on the table (Benjamin suggests) and, with a complementary gesture, politicise art. The fact that, however, Benjamin wrote this about Marinetti while being much more lenient towards a great poet as Baudelaire shows how many complicated knots intertwine in the phenomenon of poetic license: should we no longer read *The Flowers of Evil* after what Baudelaire wrote in *My Heart Laid Bare*?

Some people – for example philosopher Berys Gaut[74] – with extreme moralism, argue that morally reprehensible works cannot be masterpieces, which would force us to give up quite a few essential works. More moderately, it could be argued that, in depicting evil, there may be different moral attitudes (Picasso's *Guernica* and *The Disasters of War* by Goya are different from the *Campaign in Russia* by Léon Degrelle). The licenses we grant *Lolita* do not apply to a soap opera. When an artist, great or minor, speaks as a commentator, s/he has no special immunity. And most importantly, a massacre will never be a masterpiece as such. If anything, a novel *about* massacres will be a masterpiece. As we read in the preface of *The Picture of Dorian Gray*: "there is no such thing as a moral or an immoral book. Books are well written, or badly written. That is all."

But there is still one point that, in conclusion, I would like to bring attention to. In the case of surprise, reality asserts its rights by contradicting our expectations and our sense of plausibility. In the same way, in the case of denial, reality suggests how problematic it is, at times, to grant poetic licenses, because maybe what we have under our eyes is reality pure and simple, without a veil of poetry, the only veil being that of convention and self-defence.

4. Derealisation.

Hence a third aspect, which concerns the postmodern period we went through in the second half of the twentieth century. It consists in claiming that 'theory' – that is, something serious – should have a paraliterary statute, halfway between rhetoric and logic, reality and fiction, mythos and logos. This was part of a project of deconstruction of the distinctions between reality and fiction, serious and non-serious, literature and philosophy. In order to focus on this point, from 1979 (the year of publication of *The Postmodern Condition*) we should flash back a hundred years and return to the *Birth of Tragedy*, which is the true archetypal text of postmodernism. The Dionysian world is just a fictional universe to which Nietzsche transposes the problems of the present, covering them up with an archaic and primal aura. Nietzsche is an opponent of the Enlightenment and rejects the idea that reason and progress bring virtue and happiness; he considers this view banal and false (and indeed it is, if we put it in the terms of the bourgeois morality of the late-nineteenth century, the one that is indeed represented by *Heart*).

Against this idea he sets a telluric and tragic-artistic world, opposed to reason – the world of Wagner, essentially (but had he lived in the sixties and seventies he would have probably taken as an example the Rolling Stones or the Doors). Then, a little bit as when a furniture-maker makes a Louis XIV style armchair look older by adding woodworm holes and the like, Nietzsche transposes this opposition to the past, the Greek past. He creates a contrast between the pre-Socratics as tragic thinkers and Socrates as a rationalist (that is, as a bourgeois and optimistic professor of the nineteenth century), who argues that knowledge and virtue go hand in hand. This is why the central point of the *Birth of Tragedy*, even more than the dialectic between Dionysian and Apollonian, is the contrast between the theoretical kind – happy to lift the veil and face the truth – and the artistic kind, who instead would pass all his time endlessly revealing and exposing, enjoying the re-veiling even more than the unveiling: "for if the artist in every unveiling of truth always cleaves with raptured eyes only to that which still remains veiled after the unveiling, the theoretical man, on the other hand, enjoys and contents himself with the cast-off veil".[75] And Nietzsche's sympathy goes all to the artist and his ride through the veils in a symphony of masks.

Here we find the origin of much postmodernism and of 'theory' mixing literature and philosophy, rhetoric and logic. The reasons for this preference for the mask and the artist are, in my opinion, easily recognizable. A professor of philology senses all the weakness of his knowledge compared to the large Wagnerian industrial productions or to the growing prestige of natural sciences, and thus invents a new role for philosophy: that of creating new values, new myths and new addressees for its own doctrines. If we read Nietzsche's letters, it is hard not to notice the care with which he prepared the graphic layout and launch of his books, or how he hoped for huge print runs and translations into all languages, just like it happens with a best-seller today. In *Ecce Homo* he narrates about himself to the public with the same self-mythisation and lack of discretion that is required today by show business. Typically, Nietzsche, just as a postmodern 'theorist' would do, addresses his books not to his colleagues, but to a wide and indeterminate mankind (basically, the same mankind that could be found in Bayreuth listening to the complete performance of the *Ring of the Nibelung*, and that would later be found in Woodstock listening to Jimi Hendrix and Janis Joplin). A mankind that has to be shocked, surprised, and loyalised with the guarantee that every single reader is the exclusive recipient of a disturbing message of wisdom: virtue is only a form of the will to power, concepts are nothing but ancient metaphors, time circularly returns, and the real world has become a myth.

This is why for Nietzsche – and for postmodern thinkers after him – the relationship between literature and philosophy is so central. *Littérature et philosophie mêlées* – Hugo's logbook written in 1834 – was the title of a special issue of Poétique in the mid seventies, and it conveys the spirit of the time better than anything else. It is not a matter of distinguishing between theory and narrative or between metaphor and concept, since philosophy (as Rorty argued) is only one kind of writing. Fine. But what about Global Warming? If we say that there are no facts, only interpretations, then Global Warming is only an interpretation too – which might be comforting at first, but in the long run does not augur well, since it is a very good excuse to leave things as they are. I chose this example out of the many possible ones (what about the credit spread? Cancer? The Holocaust?), because it is the one used by Bruno Latour, a convinced postmodernist, in an article in which he retracts his position.[76] In other words, in art you may very well be romantic, but in philosophy it is best to be cautious, otherwise you risk getting in trouble ("Monotheism of reason and heart, polytheism of imagination and art," as Hegel, Schelling and Hölderlin rightly said in the so-called first systematic program of German idealism).

In fact, if one thinks that there is no difference between theorizing and narrating, then there is a very high risk of formulating fashionable nonsense or bêtises. These are issues on which books were written, such as that by Sokal and Bricmont[77],which means that we are dealing with a sociologically relevant phenomenon. To realise this, it is enough to read a bit of the theoretical production of a few years ago, which Manuel Asensi, in a 2006 book dedicated to Tel Quel, titled *Los años salvajes de la teoria*.[78] Does it mean that those thinkers were mad? No, it means that they thought that 'theory' could also target surprise, excess and paradox, i.e. what Giambattista Marino regarded as the target of poetry: "Marvel is the poet's end" and "he who knows not how to amaze, let him be groomed." Maybe they forgot that, between one line and another, he specified: "I speak of the excellent and not of the clumsy".[79]

6

Possibility

Hylas. Dear Philonous, it's been ten years since our last encounter.[80] Do you remember? The ontological issue, Manzoni's 'metaphysical subtleties', particles making up tables and jam... Much water has flowed under the bridge!

Philonous. Water flows continuously, dear Hylas, but the river under the bridge remains the same.

Hylas. Back then we spoke about what there is and what there is not, ontology and metaphysics. Today I would like to move our focus, just a little bit, to something else: what there is and what there could be. What do you say? I will be the realist and you will be the supporter of possible worlds. Which is a contraposition, surely, but not as strong as many believe it to be.

Philonous. We most certainly agree on this. You know my motto: we are not what we could be, but we could be what we are not!

Hylas. And yet reality is often set against possibility and regarded as inherently negative, only able to resist. Now, undoubtedly the real shows itself like that. But this resistance is also a possibility. Think of this table: its resistance provides a positive possibility: that of using it as a support for cutlery or as a shelter from rain (and maybe even from rubble during an earthquake). In survival manuals they always mention this possibility or positivity of the table, which follows directly from its unamendability. Nobody would advise you to take shelter under a 'theoretical umbrella', to use an old fashioned expression. And a non-theoretical umbrella offers good shelter from rain, but not from rubble.

Philonous. Wait, one step at a time. I certainly agree when you say that it is wrong to oppose reality to possibility. Not only because the first has a resistance that determines the second; there is also the fact that the real is already soaked with possibility. Possibility – and, if you like, impossibility – is already part of what is present, real. If we are here today it means, among other things, that we can participate in certain events but not others; if our salary is what it is, it means that we can afford certain expenses and not others; if we have an appointment, it is important because from that appointment could arise certain developments. Every possibility is an opportunity. In all that exists, in everything that happens, lurk the germs of what could be and what will be, what can happen and what will happen.

Hylas. This is not very different from what I meant when talking about positive resistance. In any unamendability lie opportunities – what Gibson called 'affordances' – and even narrative plots: since we mentioned umbrellas, consider how many stories revolve around lost or found umbrellas. Derrida managed to write an entire lecture on the fragment by Nietzsche "I forgot my umbrella"...

Philonous. In fact, what you say of the table is absolutely right: we can use it in different ways, within certain limits (we cannot use it as an umbrella to shelter from a meteorite, or from a storm of criticism). But there are also resistances imposed directly by the possibilities, and not only in the sense that if something is not possible it will never be actualized. You'll probably agree that there is no need to witness an earthquake to be afraid of it, just as there is no need to experience happiness to wish for it. Although they are not actualized, possibilities play an active role in our lives, in our moods, in our judgments (and prejudices).

Hylas. However, giving too much importance to these things one may risk being unable to live, like Musil's man without qualities. He never said 'No', but he always said 'Not yet', and so he never moved a finger while the world around him was falling apart.

Philonous. Ulrich represents pathology. One can exceed in possibility just as one can exceed in realism. Even Peer Gynt got lost in daydreaming, wandering for most of the time without doing any good. The fact remains that the 'sense of possibility' is the lifeblood of philosophy, and I'm not ashamed to confess that in my case it was the reading of Musil that directed me towards this profession. Philosophers are not only concerned with how things are (they are as much as everyone else, from physicists to sociologists); they also deal with how they could be. They do not only look at the real world; philosophers look at all possible worlds, wondering about what they are. It is precisely for this reason that philosophy can be a powerful tool of empowerment, both individual and social: because our ability to work for a better world is a function of our ability to conceive of a different world – another way in which our world could be. If we just worship reality – and here I move to theoretical umbrellas – nothing new would ever happen.

Hylas. This is a delicate point. For me too, philosophy is the art of the possible; I do not set my realist stance against those who are capable of inventing possible worlds, but rather against those who merely say that the real does not exist. Or that it is an invention. In short, what Kant called 'ignava ratio', and I guarantee that there's a lot of it. For too long philosophers have been professionals of anti-realism, convinced as they were that science had taken possession of all reality, and that the only way to be philosophers consisted in declaring that reality does not exist. That said, for me it is not about worshiping reality, but about not denying it.

Philonous. In fact I'm not saying that one should deny it. God forbid. Reality is everything, literally. The anti-realism you're talking about does not convince me either, and those philosophers are much worse than the man without qualities: they do not merely say 'Not yet', they say outright 'No'. I am only saying that we cannot rely on reality as if it were a book already written.

But maybe we'll come back to this later. I think that at this point we must first clarify our ideas on the underlying issue. Tell me, Hylas: What is reality for you?

Hylas. A million dollar question, or at least a hundred taller one. For me, reality is made essentially of two things that are separate, but related. The first is what I would call 'ε-reality', meaning 'epistemological reality', what the Germans call *'Realität'*. It is the reality to which Meinong refers when he says that there is a sense in which even square circles are real, or Quine when he says that "to be is to be the value of a bound variable". The same holds for a young German philosopher, my friend Markus Gabriel, when he says that everything exists in its specific field of sense – Peer Gynt in the field of sense of dramatic fiction, atoms in the field of sense of physics – and that the only thing that doesn't exist is the everything, since there is no field of sense capable of hosting the totality of all things.

Philonous. In this case the singular would be out of place: it seems to me that there are many ε-realities, one for each field of sense. Which is to say that those are possible realities, let's say epistemically possible, unless you embrace relativism in all areas. I do not think these ε-realities are so 'hyletic' after all.

Hylas. Sure, but as we have already seen, the fact that my name is Hylas does not mean that I am unable to see how real possibilities are in our lives, how they matter, how they act, how they determine our world. In this sense, I feel very pragmatic in the sense of William James and his 'will to believe'. Despair is a very real thing, which depends on the fact that the openings of passivity are closing in front of us.

Philonous. And it is not always our fault ...

Hylas. Exactly. This is something that existentialists did not consider, thinking that possibility, as such, depends essentially on us and not on the world. There is something ironic in Sartre's saying that "we are condemned to be free": I do not see all this freedom, neither in me nor outside of me. However, the problem with ε-reality (I continue to use the singular for sake of simplicity) is that it is not enough. According to ε-reality it is not strictly possible to distinguish physical causality (A produces B) from consequential logic (from A follows B) – and this is but one example among many.

Philonous. Not sure I understand. Causality is a relation between events, things that happen; the consequentiality of facts, or if you prefer of propositions. It would be enough to be clear about this distinction.

Hylas. Yes, but to be clear about this distinction we must be able to draw a distinction between external and internal world – a distinction given by perception, unamendability, the world that exists primarily because it resists. Otherwise there would be no way to distinguish between the fictional world of Ibsen and the world of physics. It is true that in *Peer Gynt* the faithful Solveig vows to wait for our wanderer until he comes back to her in the hut, and it is true in the world of physics that material bodies attract one another with a force directly proportional to the product of their masses. But there is a difference between these two kinds of truth.

Philonous. In the sense that there is a difference between the two 'fields of sense' that determine them?

Hylas. Precisely. Fictions are one thing, facts are another. For this reason, next to ε-reality I also place ω-reality (meaning ὄντως, I use the omega just to make a distinction): namely, ontological reality, what the Germans call '*Wirklichkeit*'. It manifests itself precisely as resistance, unamendability, and even, as we said a moment ago, as possibility. In short, 'Real' for me is the combination of ε-reality and ω-reality, working together. The trick of the sceptics is to use the first (not even too imaginatively) to deny the second, but it is a futile activity, because ω-reality has no intention to be set aside.

Philonous. I have no difficulty in recognizing that what you call ω-reality can limit and restrict ε-reality. I can think of using a screwdriver as a bottle opener, but not as a glass. In a sense, your insistence on Wirklichkeit recalls Quine's criticism to his colleague Nelson Goodman, who insisted on giving the same dignity to literary worlds and the world of physics, and so ended up putting fiction on the same level as facts. In principle I agree with you as I agree with Quine. But we cannot ignore the challenge of Goodman: where do we draw the line? For me this is not the usual challenge of the sceptical philosopher, as easy to formulate as it is generic. I believe it is a matter of understanding, case by case, if and when we are faced with a resistance – an 'unamendability' – that really lies in the facts rather than in fiction, i.e. in *our* version of the facts, in our ways of describing and presenting things. Provided that these are distinct spheres, even if connected, you will agree with me that there is nothing worse than passing off as ω-real what in hindsight is only ε-real.

Hylas. And vice versa. Look, the world is full of surprises, that's the point. Wittgenstein said that the world is everything that is the case, and I would add that everything that is the case is all the more the world as it happens by surprise, in derogation of our expectations and our conceptual schemes. I already said this ten years ago quoting Hamlet: there are more things between heaven and earth than we dream of in our philosophies. Today I could repeat it with perhaps an even better quote taken, this time, from a beautiful text by Walter Siti, *Il realismo è l'impossibile* [Realism is the impossible]: "Realism, as I see it, is the anti-habit: it is the slight tear, the unexpected detail, opening a gash in our mental stereotypy – it questions for a moment what Nabokov (...) calls the 'rough compromise of the senses' and it seems to let us glimpse the thing itself, the infinite reality, formless and unpredictable". Fiction is a leisurely activity; possible worlds can just be lazy variants of the real world. Reality, ω-reality, in this case, often surprises us for its improbability or cruelty. To make an example linked to these days, who would have been able to imagine even remotely the literary farce of Berlusconi?

Philonous. Few. But this is precisely the problem: if our capacity for imagination is so poor, it means that our sense of possibility is severely limited. And when you find yourself with a reality that you had not even contemplated – when ω-reality does not match any ε-reality – it's hard to come to terms with it, because you are unprepared. In my opinion this is the deep meaning of Hamlet's admonition: between heaven and earth there are a lot of possibilities that our philosophies (and our politics) cannot even imagine. Emphasizing the importance of our conceptual schemes does not mean treating them – provincial as they are – as unamendable, otherwise we would bid opportunities farewell. Of course, the opposite is also true, and here I quote Lichtenberg: there are philosophies (and politics) that have imagined things that are neither in heaven nor on earth.

Hylas. Indeed.

Philonous. So the key question concerns the interaction between ω-reality and ε-reality. As I said, for me one should be very careful not to mistake the second for the first, and I fear that in many cases we tend to do just that. In many cases we want to take for objective or natural some 'resistances', as you call them, that actually reside primarily in our heads and in our practices, let's say in our conceptual schemes, and therefore ultimately in our judgments and prejudices. Think about the rhetoric used by those opposed to relationships between people of different colour, or between persons of the same sex, stating that they are not 'natural'.

Hylas. I totally agree: honour to Foucault, Derrida and Deleuze, heroes of my twenties, as Carducci said of Carlo Alberto. I grew up in the belief that the so-called natural is often cultural in disguise. All that, with time, I added to this belief, is the awareness that this statement cannot be absolutised by arguing that the natural is *always* cultural in disguise.

Philonous. I see your point, even though the heroes of my

twenties were different. Even my heroes today are different, to be honest.

Hylas. I suspect that today we have more heroes in common, and that many of them have been dead for centuries. Anyway, I agree that this is the crux of the matter. But I'm afraid I disagree on your inclination to treat all resistance as if it could be our invention, a fiction. Traffic lights and customs are introduced by us, but the people who introduce the lights and customs are rarely the same ones who then have to observe them. The world, as well as logic, sets certain limits and we cannot pretend that we have set them instead. Here I quote our friend Paolo Bozzi, the great realist psychologist and philosopher, who left us a decade ago, just when we began to discuss these things: "If there is a black rock on an island, and if all people on the island have come to believe—through elaborate experiences and intensive use of persuasion— that the rock is white, the rock is still black and those people are idiots."

Philonous. Touché. Paolo knew how to say things! Note, however, that my scepticism about the objectivity of your 'resistance' does not imply a waiver of a solid and sturdy notion of truth, as it were enough to agree on what is true and what is false. This would actually be an idiotic thing to posit. For me it is just a matter of recognizing that the truth largely reflects the categories we rely on and the conventions we decided to adopt, and these things belong to what you call ε-reality. After all, I hope you admit that the colour of a rock is not the best example of objective property.

Hylas. So you're asking me to tell you what truths (and falsehoods) do not depend on us in any way. Well, I would distinguish three types of objects. For a start, ideal objects are completely independent of us, at least if we adopt the Platonist perspective that I'm personally fond of.

Philonous. Bad start. I hope you don't think I'm a Platonist...

Hylas. No, but I am. However, let me tell the whole story. For me ideal objects, for example mathematical entities, exist and have properties independently of our practices: 2 + 2 = 4 is an autonomous truth, even if, for example, the signs by which it is expressed were invented by us. Secondly, natural objects are also independent of us. Neither humans nor dinosaurs depend on us. Sure, a sentence like 'Dinosaurs lived between the Triassic and the end of the Cretaceous' depends on the language we use in the periodizations 'Triassic' and 'Cretaceous'; but what makes it true (that is, the *fact* that dinosaurs lived in that particular period, when human beings did not exist yet) is what it is regardless of our language. Finally, there are obviously some truths that depend very heavily on us: those related to social objects. For example, that one euro equals (if I remember correctly) 1936 liras is undoubtedly a truth that we have established ourselves, but this does not make it more negotiable than others. This is both because the 'we' who established that equivalence does not correspond to neither you nor me nor anyone we know, and because the ungovernability and opacity we see in the economic world – a world in principle completely dependent on humans – are not different from what we see in the natural world.

Philonous. I want to clarify what I said: I think we do not establish any truth. We set the facts that determine certain truths rather than others. However, in principle, your tripartite division is fine by me, as I'm fine to say that natural objects are not dependent on us.

Hylas. So?

Philonous. So our disagreement concerns, if anything, the amplitude of the three categories. In particular, I believe that, if we start to get into the details, I would rank among social objects many things that you consider natural (including humans). This is where you play the game. We have learned to say that the ontological question 'What exists?' only admits one answer, that is, 'There is everything' (since it would be contradictory to suggest the existence of something that does not exist). In the same way the question 'What objects are unamendable?' can be answered at first with 'natural objects'. But just as Quine's answer to the ontological question does not solve the problem, since we may not agree on the extent of that 'everything', so the answer to our question does not solve the problem, since we may not agree on the extension of 'natural'.

Hylas. But in this way you're unfair to the very concept of 'natural'. It is not something we can agree on – this contradicts the idea of naturality itself.

Philonous. Do you know another way to establish the extension of this term?

Hylas. The attention to objects corresponds to the primordial need to recognize obstacles and locate prey. To talk about natural objects – including humans – is not a way to pass off fictitious conventions as objective facts; it is a good approximation for an effective, economical, robust solution to the problems of survival that I mentioned at the beginning. I would say that is the only reasonable approximation. It is ω-reality: that world full of things of medium size that do not change and cannot be amended, hitting and binding us, placing constraints and offering possibilities.

Philonous. I see the point. But what you've just offered is an argument in favour of a certain way of drawing the line of demarcation, a certain way of determining what falls under the category of natural. And as you know I have serious doubts about it. For me our primordial need for survival says a lot about how we are made, not on how the world is made. Again, that's fine to say that natural objects do not depend on us, but the game is played right here, in determining what objects fully fall under the category of 'natural'.

Hylas. If you want to say that the category of 'natural' is itself cultural, I agree. But I won't insist. It is still a good step forward, isn't it? At least we know what we should focus on in our debate.

Philonous. Indeed. After all, that's how we concluded our

discussion on the ontological question as well.

Hylas. But at least let me add this: there is no doubt that certain resistances that we believed were in the world are actually in our heads. Becoming aware of this and being able to prove it is really a great achievement, and coincides, literally, with a process of emancipation. Enlightenment, in a word, is this. However, it is not just a matter of philosophical arguments, and it is not just logic and cognitive sciences that keep me from placing everything in our head. I speak not only of dinosaurs or humans. Honestly, there are times when I wish that the moral law were only in me, and instead I have the impression that it is also outside of me, in the judgments of people, in the laws of the state, in the length of my life and that of others. And even if I were given the opportunity to commit an immoral act with the assurance that no one would ever know it, I'm not so sure that I would commit it (obviously, I'm not sure of the contrary either). Why? Because I would think it would be unfair, I would have remorse, etc. These things are undoubtedly located in the head and not in the foot, but they do not depend entirely on me, but rather on a great and powerful 'we' that is in me, of which for the most part I am not conscious. So, long story short: even when it comes to what apparently is only in my head, liberation is not so easy. The clients of psychoanalysts know something about this.

Philonius. Who would have thought you were so passionate about this topic! And I really appreciate the spirit of these considerations of yours, Hylas. Moral weakness is an evil beast. Probably when it comes to interacting with the world around us and to deal with our conscience you and I are driven by the same scruples and by the same values. The differences relate to the underlying metaphysics. For you there are a few things that only reside in our heads; for me they are the vast majority (provided that we mean those things whose conditions of identity depend on our categories and our practices; we are certainly not talking about imaginary objects, as in the case of literary fiction). When

I say that humans are among the latter, I have in mind for example the debates on abortion and euthanasia, which I think demonstrate how the world itself decides neither the beginning nor the end of our lives: *we* decide, and as much as we can rely on biological science, the criteria by which to make this decision are an expression of our beliefs, our convictions, our theories. Moreover it is said that it is difficult to define what 'life' is. And as you know, I would make a similar argument also with respect to the identity of human beings, meaning our terms of persistence over time change. In this regard Hume spoke literally of 'fiction', denying the existence of an objective link between our temporal phases, and I think he had a point. And then for you it is important that the moral law be an external foundation, in the reality of things, while for me it is important to recognize that its basis lays first and foremost in our agreements and collective choices. It seems more than enough to protect it from the 'anything goes' ideology of those who do what they want, when they want. This is because the constraints imposed by membership in a community are no less important than those imposed by membership in the natural world, provided that one recognizes its importance. As you suggested about the economy. The difference is that if we find out that those constraints are wrong, if the community evolves and we realize that we have drawn the lines in the wrong places, then we can change them and assume all responsibility for it (rather than blaming the world). We can do this because it is we that make the constraints, the lines, ourselves.

Hylas. But the world will not let you draw the lines where you want. We said it before: reality circumscribes the possibilities.

Philonous. And on this I still agree. It is only a matter of understanding where and how. And I also agree on what you said earlier: breaking free from the things that are in our heads and in our practices is not easy. Psychoanalysis shows this, and even politics!

Hylas. I still do not understand how you can move so easily from one domain to another. I've already said it many times: your conventionalism is like pre-Kantian empiricism. At this rate you'll end up denying the existence of substantial differences between the laws of nature and the economy. More: between the laws of nature and timetables!

Philonous. But timetables are not drawn at random, or so we hope. They are born out of the need to solve, in a conventional but effective manner, coordination problems that are far from trivial, and which may seriously interfere with our activities. From my conventionalism it does not follow that all biological taxonomies (for example) are on the same level: it is obvious that some are better than others, and are better just because they better support the 'laws' that govern the coordination game of biology (variation, selection, organic evolution, population growth, and so on).

Hylas. Very well. However, it is this diversity in terms of efficiency that I think you cannot explain in purely pragmatic or conventional terms, without appealing directly to the structure of reality (and I obviously mean ω-reality). This is what makes the difference.

Philonous. I know. But of course I say that the burden of proof is on you, not me. Linnaeus' *Systema Naturae* – the bible of all classic taxonomies – was steeped in realist essentialism, and the result is that there was no place for the platypus. Darwin, by contrast, did not hesitate to say that 'species' is a term "arbitrarily given for the sake of convenienceto a set of individuals closely resembling each other" (his words). You will agree with me that his theory works a bit better.

Hylas. I think that there is still much to discuss... But I would say that we have taken another big step forward. Now we know that it is a matter of reasoning case by case. Am I wrong?

Philonous. You're not wrong. It certainly is not a trivial matter. Where do you want to start? I propose to set aside screwdrivers and dinosaurs and start from something less important. Do you want to talk about my colour blindness?

Hylas. No, because I know that you will try to convince me that I am the colour-blind one... Let's talk about *Peer Gynt*. Tell me, Philonous: do you think it is true that Solveig is the symbol of redeeming love?

Philonous. A million dollar question, or even a million euro one...

Notes

1. Cf. Hilary Putnam, "The Meaning of Meaning." In *Philosophical Papers: Mind, Language and Reality*, Volume II. (Cambridge, Mass: Cambridge University Press, 1975), pp. 215-271. The reference to the meaning in the world is on page 227.

2. Jacques Lacan, *The Seminar of Jacques Lacan, Book III: The Psychoses*. Edited by Jacques-Alain Miller. (New York: Norton, 1993.)

3. Plato, *Phaedo*, 118 B.

4. Umberto Eco, "Di un realismo negativo." In Mario De Caro and Maurizio Ferraris (eds.), *Bentornata realtà*. (Torino: Einaudi, 2012), pp. 91-112.

5. Claes von Hoften and Elisabeth S. Spelke, "Object Perception and Objectdirected Reaching in Infancy." In *Journal of Experimental Psychology: General*, 114, 1985, pp. 198-211.

6. James Jerome Gibson, *The Ecological Approach to Visual Perception*. (Boston: Houghton Mifflin, 1979.)

7. Johann Gottlieb Fichte, *Grundlage des Naturrechts* ("Zweiter Lehrsatz"), vol. I/3. (Stuttgart Bad Cannstatt, Frommann-Holzboog: Gesamtausgabe der bayerischen Akademie der Wissenschaften, 1796), ch. 1, § 3, pp. 342351.

8. Bert Hölldobler and Edward O. Wilson, *The Superorganism: The Beauty, Elegance, and Strangeness of Insect Societies*. (New York: W.W. Norton & C., 2008.)

9. David Rapport Lachterman, *The Ethics of Geometry: A Genealogy of Modernity*. (London: Routledge, 1989.)

10. As Rorty posited: 'But none of us antirepresentationalists have ever doubted that most things in the universe are causally independent of us. What we question is whether they are representationally independent of us'. Richard

Rorty, 'Charles Taylor on truth', in R. Rorty, *Truth and Progress, Philosophical Papers*, vol. III (Cambridge: Cambridge University Press, 1998), p. 86.

11. Putnam, *Representational Reality*. (Cambridge, Mass: MIT Press, 1988), p.114.

12. The term was coined by Quentin Meillassoux, *After Finitude*. (London: Continuum, 2008.)

13. As argued by Diego Marconi in "Realismo minimale". In Mario De Caro and Maurizio Ferraris (eds.), *Bentornata realtà*, pp. 113-137.

14. As it was defined by Quentin Meillassoux in *After Finitude*. See also Markus Gabriel, *Il senso dell'esistenza*. (Roma: Carocci, 2012.)

15. See my *Documentality. Why It Is Necessary to Leave Traces* (New York: Fordham University Press, 2012.)

16. Immanuel Kant, *Critique of Pure Reason*, A 97.

17. Daniel C. Dennett, "Darwin's 'Strange Inversion of Reasoning.'" In *Proceedings of the National Academy of Science of United States of America*, Volume 106, supplement 1 (16 June 2009), pp. 10061-10065.

18. As I explained in my *Documentality*.

19. Thomas Nagel, *Mind and Cosmos: Why the Materialist Neo-Darwinian Conception of Nature is Almost Certainly False*. (Oxford: Oxford University Press, 2012.)

20. Nagel, "What Is It Like To Be A Bat?" *Philosophical* Review 83/4, 1974, pp. 435–450.

21. Gottfried Wilhelm Leibniz, *Discourse de Metaphysique*, § 19.

22. Hans Georg Gadamer, *Truth and Method*. (London: Continuum, 2004), p. 470.

23. 'Il n'y a pas de horstexte', literally (and asemantically) "there is no outsidetext", see Jacques Derrida, *De la grammatologie*. (Paris: Les Éditions de Minuit, 1967). English translation: *Of Grammatology*, (Baltimore: JHU Press, 1998), p. 58.

24. Donald Davidson, *Inquiries into Truth and Interpretation*.

(Oxford: Oxford University Press, 1984.)

25. Nelson Goodman, *Ways of Worldmaking*. (Indianapolis: Hackett, 1978.)

26. See John McDowell, *Mind and World*. (Cambridge, Mass.: Harvard University Press, 1994.) For a criticism to this, I refer the reader to my "Mente e mondo o scienza ed esperienza?" In *Rivista di estetica*, n.s., 12, 2000, pp. 377.

27. Georg Wilhelm Friedrich Hegel, *Phenomenology of Spirit*.

28. Renée Descartes, *Meditationes de prima philosophia*. (Paris: Michel Soly, 1641.)

29. John L. Austin, *Sense and Sensibilia*. Edited by G. J. Warnock. (Oxford: Oxford University Press, 1962), p. 27.

30. Kant, *Critique of Pure Reason*, A I, B I.

31. David Hume, *A Treatise of Human Nature*. (London: John Noon, 1739), p. 40.

32. William Shakespeare, *Hamlet*, I lines 189-190: "The time is out of joint: O cursed spite I That ever I was born to set it right!"

33. Austin, *Sense and Sensibilia*, p. 105.

34. I refer the reader back to my *Il mondo esterno* (Milano: Bompiani, 2001) and *Goodbye Kant! What Still Stands of the Critique of Pure Reason*. (New York: SUNY Press, 2013.)

35. Kant, *Critique of Pure Reason*, A 51 / B 75.

36. Thomas Kuhn, *The Structure of Scientific Revolutions* (Chicago, IL: University of Chicago Press, 1962.)

37. I have articulated the distinction between natural, social and ideal objects in *Documentaliy*.

38. Karl Raimund Popper, *Logik der Forschung*. (Vienna: Julius Springer, 1935.)

39. Paolo Bozzi, *Fisica ingenua*. (Milano: Garzanti, 1990.)

40. Putnam, "Sense, nonsense and the senses. An inquiry into the powers of the human mind." In *The Journal of Philosophy*, 91/9, 1994, pp. 445–517. Reid, James, Husserl, Wittgenstein and Austin are also related to naive realism.

41. For the notion of unamendability, see my *Manifesto of New Realism*. (New York: SUNY Press, 2014.)

42. See also Gareth Evans, *The Varieties of Reference*. (Oxford: Oxford University Press, 1984.)

43. Following one of Wittgenstein's intuitions, I analysed this circumstance in my *Documentality*.

44. Markus Gabriel, *Warum es die Welt nicht gibt* (Berlin: Ullstein, 2013.)

45. See my *Manifesto of New Realism*. (New York: SUNY Press, 2014.)

46. Wilhem V.O. Quine, "Designation and existence." In *Journal of Philosophy*, 36 (26) 1939: 701709. See p. 798: "Here then are five ways of saying the same thing: 'There is such a thing as appendicitis'; 'The word *appendicitis* designates'; 'The word *appendicitis* is a name'; 'The word *appendicitis* is a substituted for a variable'; 'The disease appendicitis is a value of a variable'. The universe of entities is the range of values of variables. To be is to be the value of a variable."

47. Quine, "Whitehead and the Rise of Modern Logic." In *Selected Logic Papers*. (New York: Random House, 1966), pp. 3-36.

48. Aristotle, *Metaphysics*. IV. 2, 1003 a 33.

49. As I extensively discussed in the first part of my *Documentality*.

50. Alexius Von Meinong, "The Theory of Objects." In *Realism and the Background of Phenomenology*. Edited by Roderick Chisholm. (Atascadero, CA: Ridgeview, 1981), pp.76117.

51. Edwin B. Holt, Walter T. Marvin, William P. Montague et alii, *The New Realism: Cooperative Studies in Philosophy*. (New York: The Macmillan Company, 1912.)

53. See Graham Harman, *Guerrilla Metaphysics. Phenomenology and the Carpentry of Things*. (Chicago: Open Court, 2005); Id., *The Quadruple Object*. (London: Zero Books, 2010); Roy Bhaskar, *A Realist Theory of Science*. (London: Routledge,

2008); Levi R. Bryant, *The Democracy of Objects*. (Ann Arbor: Open Humanities Press, 2011); and, following a separate path, Tristan Garcia, *Forme et objet*. (Paris: Presses Universitaires de France, 2011.)

54. Lucy Allais, "Kant's Idealism and the Secondary Quality Analogy." In *Journal of the History of Philosophy*, 45, no. 3 (July 2007), pp. 459484.

55. Kant, *Critique of Pure Reason*, B 6970.A

56. *Ibid.* A 100-101.

57. Peter F. Strawson, *The Bounds of Sense. An Essay on Kant's Critique of Pure Reason*. (London, Methuen; New York: Barnes & Noble, 1966.)

58. Ferraris, *Il mondo esterno*, pp. 90–91. The slipper experiment is available in English in *Documentality* and in the *Manifesto of New Realism*.

59. Putnam, *Philosophy in An Age of Science: Physics, Mathematics, and Skepticism*. Edited by Mario De Caro and David Macarthur. (Boston: Harvard UP, 2013.)

60. McDowell, *Mind and World*. (Cambridge Mass.: Harvard University Press, 1994.)

61. Putnam, '"Realismo sì o no? Sbagliava anche Russell" In *La Stampa*, 4th December 2012.

62. Putnam, *Philosophy in An Age of Science*, p. 74.

63. *Ibid.*, p. 86.

64. Gaetano Kanizsa, *Vedere e pensare*. (Bologna: Il mulino, 1991.)

65. Putnam, *The Threefold Cord: Mind, Body, and the World* (New York: Columbia University Press, 1999.)

66. I defended this as early as 2001, in my *Il mondo esterno*.

67. Putnam, "What is Mathematical Truth?" In *Philosophical Papers I*. (Cambridge: Cambridge University Press, 1975) pp. 60-78.

68. See, for instance, Q. Meillassoux, *Après la finitude. Essai sur la nécessité de la contingence* (Paris: Seuil, 2006); Ray Brassier, *Nihil Unbound. Enlightenment and Extinction* (London:

Palgrave Macmillan, 2007); G. Harman, *The Quadruple Object* (London: Zer0 Books, 2011); Iain Hamilton Grant, *Philosophies of Nature after Schelling* (New York and London: Continuum, 2006). For a global overview, see Levi Bryant, Nick Srnicek and Graham Harman (eds), *The Speculative Turn. Continental Materialism and Realism* (Melbourne: re.press, 2011). For an excellent reconstruction of the similarities and differences between my own position and speculative realism, see Sarah De Sanctis' and Vincenzo Santarcangelo's Afterword to my *Introduction to New Realism* (London: Bloomsbury, 2014.)

69. As suggested by Tim Button in *The Limits of Realism*. (Oxford: Oxford University Press, 2013). We have to locate ourselves between external realism (ontology) and internal realism (epistemology), but we do not know at what exact point. If we knew, I believe we would have absolute knowledge.

70. Walter Siti, *Il realismo è l'impossibile*. (Roma: Nottetempo 2013.)

71. It is not by chance that Terence Parsons, in *Nonexistent Objects*, (New Haven and London: Yale University Press, 1980) speaks of "imported objects".

72. For an interesting exposition of the debate in analytic philosophy, see *Conceivability and Possibility*. Edited by Tamar Gendler and John Hawthorne. (Oxford: Oxford University Press 2002.)

73. Charles Baudelaire, *Œuvres complètes*, I (Paris: Bibliotèque de la Pléiade, 1975), p. 706.

74. Berys Gaut, *Art, Emotion and Ethics*. (Oxford: Oxford University Press, 2007.)

75. Friedrich Nietzsche, *The Birth of Tragedy* (1872). (London: George Allen W Unwin Ltd, 1909), p.115.

76. Bruno Latour, "Why Has Critique Run out of Steam? From Matters of Fact to Matters of Concern." In *Critical Inquiry*, 30, Winter 2004, pp. 225-248.

77. Alan Sokal and Jean Bricmont. *Fashionable Nonsense*. (New York: Picador, 1998.)

78. Miguel Asensi Pérez, *Los años salvajes de la teoría*. (Valencia: Tirant lo Blanch, 2006.)

79. TN. Giambattista Marino, *La Murtoleide* (1616). The original Italian is: "E del poeta il fin la meraviglia / parlo dell'eccellente e non del goffo / Chi non sa far stupar, vada alla striglia!"

80. Maurizio Ferraris and Achille Varzi 'Che cosa c'è e che cos'è', in VV.AA, *Nous* (Lecce: Milella, 2003), pp. 81–101. See also Achille Varzi, *Il mondo messo a fuoco*. (Roma-Bari: Laterza, 2010), App. 5– 27.

Contemporary culture has eliminated both the concept of the public and the figure of the intellectual. Former public spaces – both physical and cultural – are now either derelict or colonized by advertising. A cretinous anti-intellectualism presides, cheerled by expensively educated hacks in the pay of multinational corporations who reassure their bored readers that there is no need to rouse themselves from their interpassive stupor. The informal censorship internalized and propagated by the cultural workers of late capitalism generates a banal conformity that the propaganda chiefs of Stalinism could only ever have dreamt of imposing. Zer0 Books knows that another kind of discourse – intellectual without being academic, popular without being populist – is not only possible: it is already flourishing, in the regions beyond the striplit malls of so-called mass media and the neurotically bureaucratic halls of the academy. Zer0 is committed to the idea of publishing as a making public of the intellectual. It is convinced that in the unthinking, blandly consensual culture in which we live, critical and engaged theoretical reflection is more important than ever before.

ZERO BOOKS

If this book has helped you to clarify an idea, solve a problem or extend your knowledge, you may like to read more titles from Zero Books. Recent bestsellers are:

Capitalist Realism Is there no alternative?
Mark Fisher
An analysis of the ways in which capitalism has presented itself as the only realistic political-economic system.
Paperback: November 27, 2009 978-1-84694-317-1 $14.95 £7.99.
eBook: July 1, 2012 978-1-78099-734-6 $9.99 £6.99.

The Wandering Who? A study of Jewish identity politics
Gilad Atzmon
An explosive unique crucial book tackling the issues of Jewish Identity Politics and ideology and their global influence.
Paperback: September 30, 2011 978-1-84694-875-6 $14.95 £8.99.
eBook: September 30, 2011 978-1-84694-876-3 $9.99 £6.99.

Clampdown Pop-cultural wars on class and gender
Rhian E. Jones
Class and gender in Britpop and after, and why 'chav' is a feminist issue.
Paperback: March 29, 2013 978-1-78099-708-7 $14.95 £9.99.
eBook: March 29, 2013 978-1-78099-707-0 $7.99 £4.99.

The Quadruple Object
Graham Harman
Uses a pack of playing cards to present Harman's metaphysical system of fourfold objects, including human access, Heidegger's indirect causation, panpsychism and ontography.
Paperback: July 29, 2011 978-1-84694-700-1 $16.95 £9.99.

Weird Realism Lovecraft and Philosophy
Graham Harman
As Hölderlin was to Martin Heidegger and Mallarmé to Jacques
Derrida, so is H.P. Lovecraft to the Speculative Realist philoso-
phers.
Paperback: September 28, 2012 978-1-78099-252-5 $24.95 £14.99.
eBook: September 28, 2012 978-1-78099-907-4 $9.99 £6.99.

Sweetening the Pill or How We Got Hooked on Hormonal Birth
Control
Holly Grigg-Spall
Is it really true? Has contraception liberated or oppressed women?
Paperback: September 27, 2013 978-1-78099-607-3 $22.95 £12.99.
eBook: September 27, 2013 978-1-78099-608-0 $9.99 £6.99.

Why Are We The Good Guys? Reclaiming Your Mind From The
Delusions Of Propaganda
David Cromwell
A provocative challenge to the standard ideology that Western
power is a benevolent force in the world.
Paperback: September 28, 2012 978-1-78099-365-2 $26.95 £15.99.
eBook: September 28, 2012 978-1-78099-366-9 $9.99 £6.99.

The Truth about Art Reclaiming quality
Patrick Doorly
The book traces the multiple meanings of art to their various
sources, and equips the reader to choose between them.
Paperback: August 30, 2013 978-1-78099-841-1 $32.95 £19.99.

Bells and Whistles More Speculative Realism
Graham Harman
In this diverse collection of sixteen essays, lectures, and interviews
Graham Harman lucidly explains the principles of Speculative
Realism, including his own object-oriented philosophy.

Paperback: November 29, 2013 978-1-78279-038-9 $26.95 £15.99.
eBook: November 29, 2013 978-1-78279-037-2 $9.99 £6.99.

Towards Speculative Realism: Essays and Lectures Essays and
Lectures
Graham Harman
These writings chart Harman's rise from Chicago sportswriter to
co founder of one of Europe's most promising philosophical
movements: Speculative Realism.
Paperback: November 26, 2010 978-1-84694-394-2 $16.95 £9.99.
eBook: January 1, 1970 978-1-84694-603-5 $9.99 £6.99.

Meat Market Female flesh under capitalism
Laurie Penny
A feminist dissection of women's bodies as the fleshy fulcrum of
capitalist cannibalism, whereby women are both consumers and
consumed.
Paperback: April 29, 2011 978-1-84694-521-2 $12.95 £6.99.
eBook: May 21, 2012 978-1-84694-782-7 $9.99 £6.99.

Translating Anarchy The Anarchism of Occupy Wall Street
Mark Bray
An insider's account of the anarchists who ignited Occupy Wall
Street.
Paperback: September 27, 2013 978-1-78279-126-3 $26.95 £15.99.
eBook: September 27, 2013 978-1-78279-125-6 $6.99 £4.99.

One Dimensional Woman
Nina Power
Exposes the dark heart of contemporary cultural life by
examining pornography, consumer capitalism and the ideology of
women's work.
Paperback: November 27, 2009 978-1-84694-241-9 $14.95 £7.99.
eBook: July 1, 2012 978-1-78099-737-7 $9.99 £6.99.

Dead Man Working
Carl Cederstrom, Peter Fleming
An analysis of the dead man working and the way in which capital is now colonizing life itself.
Paperback: May 25, 2012 978-1-78099-156-6 $14.95 £9.99.
eBook: June 27, 2012 978-1-78099-157-3 $9.99 £6.99.

Unpatriotic History of the Second World War
James Heartfield
The Second World War was not the Good War of legend. James Heartfield explains that both Allies and Axis powers fought for the same goals - territory, markets and natural resources.
Paperback: September 28, 2012 978-1-78099-378-2 $42.95 £23.99.
eBook: September 28, 2012 978-1-78099-379-9 $9.99 £6.99.

Find more titles at www.zero-books.net